Sheila Hughes

With degrees in medicine and theology, Dr. Hughes brings a balanced perspective to these seemingly combative topics. Finally, a book written on these issues by an expert in both fields.

–Gerry Robert, best-selling author of *The Millionaire Mindset*

At last! A breakthrough book that builds a bridge between science and religion. Lame Science and Blind Religion delivers a practical, research based, real world roadmap that leads you to a bridge of understanding the natural and supernatural of the universe.

–Sam Farina, coach, speaker, and evangelist

Earlier this afternoon I got halfway into reading of your draft and took a break to rest my eyes. In the interim I watched a movie on television -The Pursuit of Happiness with Will Smith. I don't know if you ever watched that movie but it was like God was preparing me for the last half of your book. In the movie, which was a true story, Will played the life of a black man down on his luck who by his own determination and faith in himself was able to get himself up off the streets and become a Wall Street broker. Then I read the last half of your book following the movie. I felt truly moved by your book and it was as God was connecting the dotted lines from the movie to the book. I have reread Chapters 39 and 40 again and again. Those two chapters are profound and will be to anyone who takes the time to read the entire book. You have brought all of this together by writing a good understanding of science and religion and then making it personal. Since I retired the middle of March I have thought about where I go from here. Now I feel I have something to give back and truly believe that God will lead me to it.

–Bill Cagle

LAME SCIENCE

BLIND RELIGION

LAME SCIENCE

BLIND RELIGION

Bridging the Gap between
Science & Religion

LYNN A. HUGHES
M. TH., M.D.

LIFESUCCESS PUBLISHING, LLC
8900 E. Pinnacle Peak Road, Suite D240
Scottsdale, AZ 85255

Telephone:	800.473.7134
Fax:	480.661.1014
E-mail:	admin@lifesuccesspublishing.com
ISBN:	978-1-59930-359-8

Cover:	Daniela Savone, LifeSuccess Publishing, LLC
Text:	Lloyd Arbour, LifeSuccess Publishing, LLC

Edit:	Publication Services Inc.

COMPANIES, ORGANIZATIONS, INSTITUTIONS, AND INDUSTRY PUBLICATIONS. Quantity discounts are available on bulk purchases of this book for reselling, educational purposes, subscription incentives, gifts, sponsorship, or fundraising. Special books or book excerpts can also be created to fit specific needs such as private labeling with your logo on the cover and a message from a VIP printed inside. For more information, please contact our Special Sales Department at LifeSuccess Publishing, LLC.

ACKNOWLEDGMENTS

In 1975, I first moved to Concord, North Carolina, to begin a practice of ear, nose, and throat care in Cabarrus County. A year later, I had the pleasure of going to a lecture at Rowan Technical College in Salisbury, North Carolina. That was the beginning of my interest in principles of success. Tying the principles of success to the Bible became an ongoing goal. That is when I began looking at Biblical principles from a different view.

I began studying the works of Jim Rohn to look at those who were promoting success principles that were in the Bible. I began to study these principles from a Biblical standpoint and to listen to tapes produced and sold by Nightingale Conant.

I continued to be very active in the Episcopal Church in Concord and subsequently shifted to the Assembly of God Church in Concord. As I continued to tie together my theology degree and learning in the field of medicine and science with new ways of dealing with medical care, I always had this book in mind.

Earl Nightingale was a person I wanted to meet and had planned to meet him. He had been a great influence in my search for science principles. When he died before I met him, I resolved that would not happen again. I would make the effort to meet all of the people that I thought were advanced in the area of success and in ways that related to the Bible.

Subsequently, I attended courses by Zig Ziglar, Bill Harris, Robert Schuller, Hale Dwoskin, John Maxwell, Franklin Graham, Stephen Covey, Mark Victor Hanson, Jack Canfield, Bob Proctor, and Gerry Robert. I studied Rick Warren's and Wayne Dyer's books and shared much of this with my Oklahoma Baptist University roommates, Bruce Naylor and Ralph

Faudrey. I read Bruce Wilkinson's interesting interpretation of the Old Testament in *The Prayer of Jabez*.

My wife, Sheila, helped me to move in a new direction in my life and study. She enjoyed going to Las Vegas, and we would go together to see the shows. She enjoyed games. I preferred to go to medical meetings. One year I had a problem finding a medical meeting at a time that would be good for both of us, so I elected to make a shift and took a one-week meeting with Jack Canfield. This meeting opened my eyes to a new way of looking at the possibilities of a book. While studying at this course, I learned more about quantum physics and discussed it with a fellow student. She highly recommended that I go to John Assaraf's course. This was the best course she had ever discovered related to quantum physics. I then went to Assaraf's course in San Diego in the fall and learned of phenomenal relationships between quantum physics, science, and religion. John Assaraf and his partner Murray Smith became good friends of mine and have been very helpful with this book.

I met Robert Schuller in Charlotte, and when we go to Las Vegas or Los Angeles, we make every effort to attend the Crystal Cathedral for Sunday services. He has been a major influence in the development of this book. The Biblical emphasis he uses is fantastic.

I took the first cruise that Bob Proctor sponsored and had the great opportunity to meet him and his family. I met Gerry Robert and many of the people who worked with LifeSuccess Publishing. This was the way I began working on the book *Lame Science and Blind Religion* with Hugh Nicholson, who shared many ideas. It seems as though God works in mysterious ways to move us in the direction He would have us go. During the second cruise I attended with Bob Proctor, I had the pleasure to meet Peggy McColl, who directed me in the writing of the book and taught me the best ways to promote sales in order to share the book with as many people as possible.

I also want to thank Sam Farina for being my friend and assisting me in writing this book. He is a great Biblical scholar and an excellent minister in the Assembly of God Church.

My wife, Sheila, has provided great support for all the work a book requires. I want to thank my daughter, Shannon Williams, who did writing in college and has a masters degree from William and Mary. She has been helping with the writing of the book. My daughter, Heather Griswold, did some of the research, making the book possible. My computer expert, Dianne Biggerstaff, worked diligently as needed to transcribe my thoughts for this book.

DEDICATION

In this dedication, I share my wonderful parents, Ross and Pauline Hughes, who gave their lives to their children without any regret. Training, teaching, traveling, and being open to who their children—Joe, Janet, John, and Lynn—would be by helping, teaching, and answering questions. Dad taught us how to build churches in two ways—structure and heart. Building a church and a family was his goal. Mother's goal was to have a loving family. Their goal was to share in the world by helping others regardless of race and creed, always providing an emphasis on love and sharing. Dad never wrote his book, *How to Build Churches*. He spoke about it and lectured about it, but never wrote it. Mother forever supported his work and direction. I write this book for them to be remembered for what they did for others, to honor all they shared without writing it down. I want to leave my part of their legacy in a book they would be proud to share.

FOREWORD

Many people today are intrigued with the thought that our engrained beliefs may not be correct. This is especially true for those who are questioning their religious beliefs. Religion has long been untouchable for many people, as they have been convinced that the truths they were taught as a child were absolute. Today many of those truths have been called into question by the quest for discovery in science as well as the quest for internal growth and development.

Dr. Hughes confronts this dichotomy in *Lame Science, Blind Religion.* By highlighting some of the core beliefs of Christianity without all the doctrine and denominational noise, Dr. Hughes offers insight and inclusion for all those searching for their own truth. We were endowed with a mind and charged with seeking our own truth. This means exploring beyond the paradigms you were taught about belief as a child and discovering anew your own path to faith.

Lame Science, Blind Religion is a pathway to lead you from the lackluster results and frustration you are currently experiencing to the abundance you deserve. When you expand the awareness of your mind, you explore your own creative potential where all your power resides. I have spent the last 40 years encouraging people to let go of their old paradigms and embark upon a fabulous world of self-discovery, and this book is an excellent way to challenge some of the most engrained ideas.

We all move through our daily lives often forgetting we have a choice—to continue on autopilot as we did the day before or to heighten the awareness of our potential and seek to find our own inner truth. I encourage you to open your mind and ask the hard questions that bring you to your greatest understanding of life and of our human existence.

—Bob Proctor, best-selling author of *You Were Born Rich*

CONTENTS

INTRODUCTION

God directed my life into thirds. My first 35 years consisted of my education—formally, informally, and spiritually. The next phase involved my searching for and finding my purpose. For me it came as a career in medicine, complemented with religious ministry. My third 35 years saw me able to pull it all together and share God's blessing for my life, not only in my medical practice—evolving and ministering as a physician to the less fortunate in the Dominican Republic, but also to my contemporaries in faith and spirituality.

I believe I have a unique and profound take on the teachings of our Lord Jesus Christ, but I also would like to share with my reader my understanding of the teachings of Christianity and how they are not contrary to a life of abundance and happiness. Jesus suffered so that we do not have to. We have had information handed to us throughout the ages that supports his message of love. I aim to bring a new awareness to Christians on this topic and invite you to join me in a life of abundant happiness, gratitude, and servitude to our fellow humans, which is the way in which we truly serve our Creator.

I had been able to do mission work and volunteer surgery 7 to 14 days per year for 17 years in the Dominican Republic near the Haitian border. I have many close Dominican friends, and there are plans for a new mission hospital in the next few years. God has recently called me to use the ability he has given me to be able to make the complex understandable to anyone. There is a dire need for meditation and prayer so that each of us can know God and his mission for each of us in his world.

In my two careers, I tried to make simple understanding of complex disease. Now in my new career, I plan to simplify the new science and how it applies to the spiritual world.

God has looked after me well, and I am grateful. Through my father and mother, he provided skills to permit me to pay for my own education with only $500 debt when I finished medical school. He saved me from fighting in Vietnam, though I served as a healer and medical doctor. He gave me travel experience through my family, the United States government, the Air Force, and the State Department, and mission work in the Dominican Republic. He provided a great experience in the Baptist Church, the Episcopal Church, and now the Assembly of God Church. He is currently opening doors for study and opportunities to share what he has done for my family and me.

Has it been a bed of roses? Yes, but with a few thorns along the way—the first two thirds. I am looking to a grand finale at 105, which may be a beginning of my next 35 years, and whatever he has in mind for me those years! "All things work for good for those who love God" (NIV Romans 8:28).

What's your plan for the next third of your life? We can all expect to live to be 80 to 85 to 95 years old. Many more people are becoming older and older before death. God has a use for you and a plan for your life during that period of time, just as he has a plan for my life. Have you considered what you can do for others? What can you do to share yourself and your life and to find God's mission for you? Think about it. Talk to others about it. What is your passion? What are your God-given skills? Ask and you shall receive a mission for the next 35 years, as in my case.

This book is your beginning. Initially, we begin with the current status of the Christian faith and then move to the time of Christ with a study of the Essenes and the Dead Sea Scrolls. We then move to the beginnings of the Christian faith. We then begin with the role of science with an introduction on theologians—science and religion working together as God provides his way for each of us. I introduce the seven laws of nature as we move through the book, which illustrate the way our brains work to help us understand how to change to be who God has created us to be. The end of the book discusses being open to change by being open to God's passion, purpose, mission, and goals as we fulfill our Creator's plan for our lives.

Let us begin with a prayer.

Father, I am thankful for this opportunity to share what you have done in my life. I am thankful for your guidance and direction. I am grateful for the continued protection you have given me in unknown ways throughout my life. Help me to recognize your need for me to fulfill your plan for my life. God works his mission for me through me. Help me be open and amenable in order to fulfill my part of your great mission. Please guide everyone reading this book to create their lives with the help of our Creator.

AMEN

CHAPTER 1

SO MANY CHRISTIAN GROUPS,
BUT WHICH IS RIGHT?

> *You must be the change you want to see in the world.*
>
> **–Gandhi**

The Christian world is in crisis for membership. A survey dated February 25, 2008, by the Pew Forum on Religion and Public Life (www.pewforum.com) on the changing demographics of Christianity in the United States claims that today "nearly half of American adults [are] leaving the faith tradition of their upbringing to either switch allegiances or abandon religious affiliation altogether." This study was conducted by interviews with more than 35,000 adults to document a diverse and dynamic U.S. religious population. Much of the study confirms earlier findings—mainline Protestant churches are in decline, non-denominational churches are gaining, and the ranks of the unaffiliated are growing. I would like to examine, in this book, some of the reasons for this decline. Why hasn't mainstream Christianity kept pace with the rapidly changing understanding of God's world in which we live?

Early Christian church "father," Bishop Augustine of Hippo (AD 354–430), St. Augustine to Catholics, stated, "God will only reveal to man what he is capable of understanding." Or, "When man is ready, God provides the answers." (orthodoxwiki.org) To this I may add, it is time that Christian church leaders of all types merge the understanding of the world we have from science—all forms of it—with the spiritual principles taught by Jesus of Nazareth—the Christ. If a shift in understanding and teachings does not occur, I fear the trend of a declining Christian population is inevitable.

Much of my aim here is to help the individual gain a greater understanding of God's world and to shed the light on how it is possible and necessary to accomplish the merging in order to grow as Christians. I hope to solidify the faith of my reader, and not turn him or her from the teachings of their faith of choice. There is so much more available to us now to assist us in more fully comprehending the messages of Jesus Christ and the Creator God's development of our universe.

The previously mentioned study by the Pew Forum goes on to describe the phenomenon of the shifting U.S. religious demographics as such: "The American religious economy is like a marketplace—very dynamic, very competitive. Everyone is losing, everyone is gaining. There are net winners and losers, but no one can stand still. Those groups that are losing significant numbers have to recoup them to stay vibrant." This phenomenon of ever-changing movement is not particular to marketplaces, but it is inherent in all activity or states of consciousness for humans. This is a good example of a "super law," which applies scientific understanding of natural laws to spiritual principles, called The Law of Perpetual Transmutation of Energy. This tells us that everything is energy and energy is always in motion. Therefore, nothing in life, in our universe, remains stationary. Everything changes, and without change and a greater understanding of our surroundings and how we "fit," we will actually work against some natural laws. Failure to acknowledge the validity of these laws is like failing to acknowledge that gravity exists. If you don't respect gravity, you're in for a tough time in life.

Throughout this book, I will introduce and expand upon the seven super laws of the universe, but I'll mention a few now. As I said earlier, super law number one is The Law of Perpetual Transmutation of Energy. Energy is motion. Energy never stands still. It takes one form, then another. Change is all there is. This is certainly true when applied to all life. Civilizations change. Humans change. With the constant biological process going on in us, we actually create new bodies on a cellular level every seven years. So it is becoming apparent on a grand scale that religions are also feeling this radical shift, and a greater awareness is necessary or we will certainly continue to see a decline of believers in the world.

These laws of scientific study can be applied in all areas of life to gain a better understanding of God's world, and I will use the Bible to show that these are the very same concepts taught by Jesus of Nazareth who lived over 2,000 years ago. God has been trying to communicate this to us for centuries.

Let's return briefly to the U.S. Religious Landscape Survey by the Pew Forum and look at the rapidly changing statistics to examine what is happening "in the minds of the American Christian" and, I daresay, Christians throughout the world. The survey results estimate that:

- The United States is 78 percent Christian and about to lose its status as a majority Protestant nation, at 51 percent and slipping.

- More than one quarter of American adults have left the faith of their childhood for another religion or no religion at all, the survey found. Factoring in moves from one stream or denomination of Protestantism to another, the number rises to 44 percent.

- One in four adults ages 18 to 29 claim no affiliation with a religious institution.

I contend that our fluid society is hungry for change and a greater understanding than many churches can provide. The status quo in awareness of spirituality in religion is not satisfying to the increasingly more educated populace, and our citizens are seeking to satisfy this hunger elsewhere. Yet, it can be found in the very teachings they often reject.

A good example is within the Roman Catholic Church. The Pew Forum survey found that this faith has lost more members than any other faith due to something called "affiliation swapping." This means that while nearly one in three Americans was raised Catholic, fewer than one in four say they're Catholic today. That means roughly 10 percent of all Americans are ex-Catholics. They have swapped out their Catholic tradition for a faith that they feel is more in line with their needs today. Other religions aren't immune to this type of exodus.

Protestant traditions such as Baptist and Methodist are also losing ground to non-denominational churches due to the perception that these traditions can no longer suit the needs of people today.

This book will look at these changes and show the reader how one need not abandon one's congregation in order to find a greater understanding of spirituality or of God. Each person needs to look for himself or herself and perhaps take this new awareness to the congregation and share the insight with others so that they may grow.

Who is right? Political elections are helpful in considering the human tendency to emphatically state that one point of view or another is right or wrong. We refer to things as being "black or white" or "good or bad." This actually brings to mind another super law of quantum physics. Super law number three is The Law of Relativity. Everything in our material world is made *real* by its relationship to something else (i.e., hot only exists because we compare it to cold). Relationships are everything, and everything is due to relationships with other things. As I said earlier, in subsequent chapters, I will delve further into each of these laws, but for the moment, just consider that we need this comparison to understand things by knowing what they are *not*. It is the way we grapple with observation in our mind. The tendency in us, as humans, is to choose sides, particularly in regard to religious organizations, how we arrive at what we consider "orthodoxy," or the correct way, and "heresy," the incorrect way. Many "orthodox groups," of course, then see their group and teaching to be "the only way to God."

I will ask you to abandon this mind-set in light of the law I mentioned. What if the "right way" to God exists in all people in all groups? Who gets to decide who is right anyway? And who decided in the first place?

Christians will often proudly proclaim themselves Christians, yet point out the flaws, lack of understanding (from their perspective), or downright condemn other "Christians" and non-Christians, but on whose authority?

In the following chapters, we will look at the formation of Christianity and consider the events, writings, and outcomes of historical events to see if we might gain insight into what is now a polarized society on the issues of faith. So many Christians, but which group is right?

[30]What then shall we say? That the Gentiles, who did not pursue righteousness, have obtained it, a righteousness that is by faith; [31]but Israel, who pursued a law of righteousness, has not attained it. [32]Why not? Because they pursued it not by faith but as if it were by works. They stumbled over the "stumbling stone." [33]As it is written: "See, I lay in Zion a stone that causes men to stumble and a rock that makes them fall, and the one who trusts in him will never be put to shame."

–Romans 9:30–33 (New International Version)

CHAPTER 2

THE PRE-CHRISTIAN ERA

> *Every achiever I have ever met says my life turned around when I began to believe in me.*
>
> –Robert Schuller, minister, author

If we refer the canonical gospels, those accepted as sacred by Christians and included in the 27 books that make up the New Testament, a man named Jesus of Nazareth was born of a young Jewish woman named Mary in the town of Bethlehem during the reign of Herod and under Roman secular rule. He was divinely conceived and grew up under the protection of a human stepfather, Joseph, a Jewish carpenter. Jesus was an exceptional child who could debate with scholars and doctors in the synagogue, and sometime around his thirtieth year, he began a teaching ministry that did not sit well with the Jewish authorities or those of the Roman government.

The stories of the New Testament inform us that this man used stories and metaphors to teach his followers a new way to be and a new way to understand God. In a time when Jews had been under the oppression of the Roman state and sects of Judaism sprang up to challenge the correct way to be Jewish, all assumed the end was near and would occur with a cataclysmic war that would finally bring them "King Messiah," who would liberate them as a nation and a people. They would have their kingdom on Earth.

Jesus didn't do that for most Jews. He came along to teach a different message. He taught peace and love. He taught radical ideas such as "turn the other cheek" when his society wholeheartedly accepted the idea of "an eye for an eye" as being appropriate justice. He taught messages that required the observers to use their critical thinking skills and powers of interpretation to understand the message versus being able to retort with rote answers to complex dogmatic questions. Jesus was indeed a first-century *rabbi*, which means—teacher.

So for the Jews, Jesus did not fulfill the role of messiah because he was not the political and military liberator they so desperately awaited. He was teaching nonviolent resistance in a violent world. Factions of Jews became, prior to Jesus's time, known as Zealots, whose only attachment to their faith was the determination to liberate the ethnic Jewish population from the oppression of the Romans. These were militant groups who fought. It is from them that we get the word *zealous*, meaning overly eager.

In Jesus's own life we see the other types of Jews amongst whom he grew up. In scripture, we see Jesus's familial ties to temple priests. This group was known as the Sadducees and thought that in order to be a good Jew, temple worship was necessary and all temple worship was centered on the *one* temple in Jerusalem. Dispersing of Jews from Jerusalem made this difficult when the land was seized over the centuries by invaders. Some Jews began to form congregations of men who would gather together to study Torah—the first five books of the Christian Old Testament, which are referred to in some denominations as the Books of Moses—along with the Nevi'im and the Ketuvim (The prophets and the Teachings). These groups gathered in synagogues and found that though temple worship was good, it should not be the focus of Jewish life. This group is commonly referred to as the Pharisees.

The New Testament shows us stories of Jesus in both the synagogue and the temple, but he is conspicuously absent between the ages of 12 and 30. Where did he go? What was he doing? Were there yet still other ways to *be* Jewish? The answer is yes. Though I make no claim to know the exact whereabouts of the Christian messiah from his days in the synagogue discussing Torah with the doctors (depending on the translation you use) to his arrival on the scene when beginning his ministry, there was yet another way to be Jewish in the first century AD. There were groups called Essenes scattered all about the Middle East who were communal Jews. They lived in large complexes, anxiously awaiting the coming of the messiah. They gathered and studied all types of information, and archaeological excavations have shown they did not limit their libraries to Jewish scripture. Most of what we know about the Essenes comes from ancient historians such as Flavius Josephus and Philo, and it is remarkably similar to what we know about the Qumran community from their archaeological remains and their literature. Qumran was a community unearthed by archaeologists when a young shepherd boy threw a rock and discovered earthenware jars filled with ancient scrolls in the 1940s. These documents are known today as *The Dead Sea Scrolls* and have caused quite a stir in scholarly religious communities.

The main reason that many religious leaders have feared these documents is that they were written and hidden away long before the various religions and religious beliefs we know today were created. Some feared these writings would completely upend what they believed to be true.

Christians broke away from Jewish law and tradition centuries ago, yet even today people are still searching for answers that make sense to them in their lives. It is for this reason we have seen such an exodus from mainstream religions that no longer fill the needs of their congregations. The pre-Christian era and subsequent religious upheaval was not so very different than the spiritual movement we are seeing today.

[4]Christ is the end of the law so that there may be righteousness for everyone who believes.

[5]Moses describes in this way the righteousness that is by the law: "The man who does these things will live by them."[a] [6]But the righteousness that is by faith says: "Do not say in your heart, 'Who will ascend into heaven?'[b]" (that is, to bring Christ down) [7]"or 'Who will descend into the deep?'[c]" (that is, to bring Christ up from the dead). [8]But what does it say? "The word is near you; it is in your mouth and in your heart,"[d] that is, the word of faith we are proclaiming: [9]That if you confess with your mouth, "Jesus is Lord," and believe in your heart that God raised him from the dead, you will be saved. [10]For it is with your heart that you believe and are justified, and it is with your mouth that you confess and are saved."

–Romans 10:4–10 (New International Version)

CHAPTER 3

JESUS IN TRUTH

Action makes more fortune than caution.

–Luc DeClapiers, 1715–1747

In addition to the works of the Roman historians mentioned in Chapter 2 (Josephus was a Jewish historian writing for the Romans), we have hundreds of documents surviving from the first three centuries that tell similar accounts of the life and teachings of Jesus. Many of these documents were considered heretical by early church authorities and ordered burned or destroyed, but some survived, and partial copies have continued to resurface through archaeological finds and secret libraries. Though the content and message may or may not be pure, it is exciting to see more and more support for the life of Jesus, and each depiction gives us a greater understanding of how he was seen in his day.

Consider news reports today. Depending on the stand of the reporter, we hear vastly differing accounts of the same events, and we as intelligent humans are left to decide what is accurate or not. For much of the Christian era, the opposing information was considered too dangerous to share with the average man because it would challenge the religious and subsequent political authority. We are under no such constraints today and are free to research, read, and translate any and all documents that contain information relating to our own beliefs and to draw our own conclusions.

> *Hymn 9 [DSS]: I thank Thee, O Lord, for Thou has not abandoned the fatherless or despised the poor.*

> *Hymn 18: Blessed art Thou, O my Lord, who hast given to Thy servant the knowledge of wisdom that he may comprehend Thy wonders in Thy abundant grace.*

> *Matthew 11:25: I thank you, Father, Lord of heaven and earth, because you have hidden these things from the wise and the intelligent and have revealed them to infants; yes, Father, for such was your gracious will (NRSV).*

What fantastic insights we can glean from documents heretofore kept from the reach of the average person! It is a wonderful example of how we can find truth in other teachings without believing or "buying into" everything. We now have the ability, with resources such as the Internet and ever-expanding knowledge and critical-thinking skills, to learn and decide for ourselves, for our relationship with the Father is a personal one.

Through the many historical accounts, Jesus is interesting, not in the fact that he congregated with many various groups and types of people, but that he welcomed all to a greater understanding. The various religious rules and regulations of Christian denominations we know of today didn't exist and weren't of Jesus's making. This is a very important idea to hold onto because many people don't really step back and think about the fact that they were born into the religion that they now assume, but that religion doesn't have all the answers—it can't; its man-made not divinely created.

When we view our activities and habits of belief from this perspective, it allows us to see and accept that there are many ways to faith and belief in a higher power, and not all of those come from sitting in a particular pew on Sunday.

In the next chapter, we will clearly see that Jesus had a unique message overall, yet he was truly a man among people, and his message of love remains the fundamental basis for Christian behavior and attitudes. Recognizing what Jesus did during his life, we can learn to be more like him in many more ways. One of these ways is by using his knowledge to discern truth and to reach a large and diverse audience.

[29]*The next day John saw Jesus coming toward him and said, "Look, the Lamb of God, who takes away the sin of the world!* [30]*This is the one I meant when I said, 'A man who comes after me has surpassed me because he was before me.'* [31]*I myself did not know him, but the reason I came baptizing with water was that he might be revealed to Israel."* [32]*Then John gave this testimony: "I saw the Spirit come down from heaven as a dove and remain on him.* [33]*I would not have known him, except that the one who sent me to baptize with water told me, 'The man on whom you see the Spirit come down and remain is he who will baptize with the Holy Spirit.'* [34]*I have seen and I testify that this is the Son of God."*

–John 1:29–34 (New International Version)

CHAPTER 4

THE REAL MESSAGE OF CHRIST

People are like stained-glass windows. They sparkle and shine when the sun is out, but when the darkness sets in, their true beauty is revealed only if there is a light from within.

–Dr. Elizabeth Kuebler Ross

Love is the very basis for all of Christ's teachings. In fact, in Matthew 5:43, The Sermon on the Mount, Jesus said, "You have heard that it was said, 'You shall love your neighbor and hate your enemy.' But I say to you, 'Love your enemies and pray for those who persecute you, so that you may be children of your Father in heaven.'" We have to assume that Jesus knew his followers had been taught to hate their enemies, but where was this written? It is interesting that such a statement is not found in the Old Testament, but it is found in the Dead Sea Scrolls.

Most of us are familiar with concepts such as "pray for your enemies," and yet we often still fall victim to wanting to take revenge or hold a grudge against someone. This has been a longstanding practice within human existence. It seems that it was common among Jesus's audience to feel this way. In fact, even in today's world, we all know people who despise others based on race, creed, color, religious affiliation, or some other quality we judge to be not in alignment with our concept of what is "right."

When we speak badly of others or wish bad things would happen to others, it tends to have negative repercussions against us. In the context of history, cursing was the contemplation or sending of negative thoughts toward another human. Jesus taught that we are to love and informed his disciples that if they were truly to be children of God, they were to *love* their enemies, not hate them.

Jesus, it is agreed, taught a new way of being when most of the spiritual leaders of his day were teaching the old way: "Keep to yourself, and only be amongst your own kind. Others who don't believe as we do are bad." Unfortunately, this mind-set seems to have carried on throughout the centuries. We still find it prevalent in many Christian groups today—yet we see that this is *not* what Jesus taught.

Jesus's circle was an open one, accepting all who entered and giving freely of the knowledge he possessed. In all three synoptic gospels—Matthew, Mark, and Luke—Jesus said, "Nothing is covered up that will not be uncovered, and nothing secret that will not become known. What I say to you in the dark, tell in the light; and what you hear whispered, proclaim from the housetops." Jesus wanted his doctrines to be taught to the public no matter what their affiliation at that time.

Jesus completely ignored any kind of hierarchy among men or women and taught that all individuals stand equally before God. Jesus not only welcomed women into his circle, but also taught them from the scriptures and associated with them freely, an act that flew in the face of traditional accepted restrictions on the sexes.

Jesus further crossed existing barriers by associating with those considered unclean, such as tax collectors, prostitutes, and those with illnesses and diseases thought to be a curse from God. The gospels of Mark and Matthew tell of Jesus's visit to the house of Simon the leper, and it was well-known that people in this time were very afraid of lepers.

There is a specific incident in the gospel of Luke that shows the height of Jesus's disregard for the accepted rituals of the day. In the eighth chapter of Luke, there is a story of an encounter with a woman who had been suffering from hemorrhages for 12 years. Knowing Jesus could heal her, she snuck up behind him and touched the fringe of his robe—and was immediately healed.

When Jesus asked who had touched him, her reaction was one of fear and dread. This is due to the fact that a woman bleeding was considered unclean in the law of Moses. If anyone touched anything she had touched, they were also considered unclean. Using this standard, the woman had made Jesus unclean, and he would be required to wash and then he would be unclean until evening. This is why the woman was so afraid. A rabbi would have rebuked her strongly and even punished her.

Not only did Jesus not punish her, he stated, "Daughter, your faith has made you well; go in peace" (Luke 8:48). Afterward, he did not wash, and in fact went straight to the home of Jairus, leader of the synagogue. Jesus *intentionally* crossed over the boundaries between the profane and the holy. He went straight from the unclean sinner into the house of a synagogue leader, spreading uncleanness everywhere. The reason, of course, is that Jesus rewrote the rules about purity and impurity. In Mark 7, Jesus clearly teaches that no external object can render a person unclean; rather, "It is what comes *out* of a person that defiles. For it is from *within*, from the human heart, that evil intentions come." Jesus persisted in tearing down the artificial barriers erected by other religious leaders and in creating an all-inclusive faith that preached love and acceptance over hatred and fear.

So again I ask: why does this matter? It matters for many reasons, but mostly because we are learning constantly, and at a higher pace than ever before, about the real world in which Jesus lived. Our understanding of his surroundings is becoming clearer. We can see that the people of his time were not in agreement religiously, even if they called themselves Jews. Like the Christian movement that follows the death of Jesus of Nazareth, Jews of his time were not united in an understanding of God, their own scriptures, or their world. In effect, they had their own various denominations of Judaism, and it is in this atmosphere that early Christianity emerged.

43 You have heard that it was said, "Love your neighbor[a] and hate your enemy." 44But I tell you: Love your enemies[b] and pray for those who persecute you, 45that you may be sons of your Father in heaven. He causes his sun to rise on the evil and the good, and sends rain on the righteous and the unrighteous. 46If you love those who love you, what reward will you get? Are not even the tax collectors doing that? 47And if you greet only your brothers, what are you doing more than others? Do not even pagans do that?

–Matthew 5:43–47 (New International Version)

CHAPTER 5

THE FIRST CHRISTIANS

> *Obstacles cannot stop you, problems cannot stop you, and most of all, other people can't stop you. Only you can stop you.*
>
> **–Jeffrey Gitomer, author and sales trainer**

A benefit to reading the often-labeled "heretical texts" is that we can find some common threads that further point to the value of the accepted books contained in the New Testament. Validation of the stories occurs when we compare the teachings, though some vary widely. We can use them, at minimum, to see that the historical figure of Jesus was indeed a person who lived around this time.

But once he was gone, his followers had their "notes" from class with Jesus, and many different opinions regarding who he was, how he lived and loved, and what he meant by his teachings multiplied exponentially. Within a short time, many followers of Jesus of Nazareth had their own groups or congregations, and there was no unity among Christians throughout the emerging Christendom. In his 2003 book titled *The Lost Christianities*, University of North Carolina professor Bart D. Ehrman tells us that "the wide diversity of early Christianity must be seen above all in the theological beliefs embraced by people who understood themselves to be followers of Jesus."

Ehrman goes on to explain that by the second and third centuries, many Christians believed in one God, while others believe there were 2, or 30, or as many as 365! Their views of creation and benevolence or malevolence of the Creator also varied widely.

I think it is safe to say that the divided Christian community is not a new phenomenon. Christianity arose in a religiously and politically divided era, and it was only by the iron-fist rule of Constantine in the fourth century that the Church united (and separated at the same time) when he called the Council of Nicea in AD 325. This made it possible for church fathers to state with authority what was orthodoxy and what was heresy. And they could also penalize those who disagreed—often with very painful death and torture.

That united church lasted, with its own set of problems and struggles, until it exploded from the weight of oppression from a theocratic Christendom with the pope taking authority only from God and being superior to even the Holy Roman Emperor—a coup pulled off with the coronation of Charlemagne by Pope Leo III in AD 800. This made it quite easy for the church to control and stamp out, with the backing of secular authority, any new religious movements or deviant ways of thinking about religion, spirituality, and even scientific understanding of the world. One of the Catholic Church's "crusades" was against a group of Christians called "Cathars," which existed mostly in Southern France.

Martin Luther, in the sixteenth century, challenged the Catholic Church's selling of salvation via plenary indulgences at a time when technological advances had produced the Gutenberg press, allowing for the rapid perpetuation of ideas. People learned to read. When they learned to read, they learned to explore the world around them, and they found they were not always being fed the truth. Science began to explain things when Copernicus, Galileo, Newton, and others realized that there is more to this universe than we know, and its arrangement did not reflect that which is described in Genesis. So began the journey to *enlightenment*, which is the term to describe the era that follows the medieval period, but we then learned, after several hundred years, that science can't explain it all either. In the words of the late, great Albert Einstein, "Science without religion is lame. Religion without science is blind."

Today, we are back where the early Christians found themselves. We have great information, but we just don't know how to use it. Albert Einstein and Maxwell Planck, over the past 150 years, made discoveries in science and therefore found new ways to apply old principles, or universal truths, to help us understand what some consider inexplicable. That is changing rapidly, however, as a new group of thinkers such as John Assaraf, Murray Smith, Bob Proctor, and many others have learned, and are teaching to us, how to integrate the laws of the universe with our evolving understanding of God's world.

¹¹But you, man of God, flee from all this, and pursue righteousness, godliness, faith, love, endurance and gentleness. ¹²Fight the good fight of the faith. Take hold of the eternal life to which you were called when you made your good confession in the presence of many witnesses.

–1 Timothy 6:11–12 (New International Version)

CHAPTER 6

THE CHRISTIAN QUESTION

I think I began learning long ago that those who are happiest are those who do the most for others.

–Booker T. Washington, 1856–1915, educator and author

There are many stages in life when we are filled with more questions than we can find answers to no matter where we turn. It is the very nature of childhood to ask questions in order to comprehend the natural world around us, to help us arrive at what is good, learn to avoid that which will harm us, and to help us identify the things we see. Our questions grow from simple what, why, and how questions to those requiring more thought and effort to formulate the question itself, ergo more response and information coming from the authority to whom we pose our inquiries.

Questions are also important for the spiritual journey. As stated earlier, questions require answers, which lead to greater understanding, and also, they then lead to *other questions* as we grow. To stop questioning or wondering will lead to spiritual and emotional stagnation. Nothing in nature is static. Everything remains in flux in order to achieve its most vibrant state. Blood flows. Water flows. A plant continues to grow and blossom. When the growth stops, so does the plant life. Though we cannot always see the growth of trees on a daily basis, over the course of the year, we can see its growth surpass the rooftop; we watch its yearly blooms, the filling out with leaves, the loss of leaves, the quiet time of winter, only to see it reblossom in spring. But these are the observations of the human adult. It is the same with one on a spiritual journey. Questions are the keys to creating the flow of spiritual life and provide the nourishment, just as the sun, air, water, and soil feed the tree.

No matter where your journey is beginning, know that there are questions perfectly acceptable and appropriate for you, for your personal growth and relationship with God at this time in your life on this particular journey— your journey to know the divine. Questions are the best way to grow to be able to answer from your own perspective. And your perspective of your Creator is the only one that matters.

Spirituality is indeed a personal relationship with God, our Creator. It is an individual relationship, knowledge of God that is personal and can be shared and learned for creating your direction in life. Your direction is not meant for others. Direct your contact with God, not to establish your own religion, but to develop a good relationship with God that will help you understand your purpose in this world—your mission.

The term *mission* is commonplace in Christianity as many devout members of various denominations "go on missions." The Church of Jesus Christ of Latter Day Saints is famous for its missionaries, easily identifiable in dark pants, dress shirts, and ties, peddling around town or on back country roads on bicycles, taking their church's teachings to the world. Methodists, Baptists, Catholics, Presbyterians, and all other denominations have missions or missionary work guided by the established church as well. But these are not the only way to be a missionary. In fact, I would suggest that finding a true mission, or a calling, is a lifelong process, and one that requires attention to the signs that the Almighty sends to each of us as to how best to serve him by serving humanity. We are all called to do different work, and each of us may do different missions within this one lifetime. It requires attention to your relationship with God to recognize this, and we can take our example by going back to the beginning—to one of the earliest Christian missionaries, Paul.

Paul the apostle, often referred to as the "apostle to the Gentiles (non-Jews), lived around AD 67 and was one of the most notable early Christian missionaries. Unlike the original 12 apostles, there is no indication that Paul ever met Jesus before the crucifixion. According to the book of Acts, his conversion took place as he was traveling the road to Damascus, where he experienced a vision of the resurrected Jesus. Paul claims that he received the gospel, or the "good news," not from man, but by "the revelation of Jesus Christ" in the form of the resurrected Christ.

Fourteen epistles, or letters, in the New Testament are traditionally attributed to Paul, although in some cases the authorship is disputed. This is indeed over half of the 27 books included in this section of the Holy Bible, which covers the teachings of the messiah. But scholars do agree that most of the teachings are attributed to him. His value as a missionary and proselyte of early Christianity is without question.

Paul's influence on Christian thinking is arguably more significant than any other New Testament author, including those who were within the inner circle of Jesus. Perhaps it is due to the nature of his writings. Paul helped early Christians put the teachings of Jesus into a usable form. He helped Christians apply the teachings in their lives versus repeating the biography and stories or parables told by Christ. Likewise, I am now applying science to Christian teachings and to religion in general.

Paul's influence on the orthodox and therefore surviving strands of Christian thought has been considerable, and he has been cited by some of the greatest theologians and apologists of all time including (St.) Augustine of Hippo (fourth and fifth century AD), Martin Luther (sixteenth century), John Calvin (sixteenth century), the Jesuit theologians, including Ignatius, and even to the German church of the twentieth century through the writings of the scholar Karl Barth, whose commentary on the Letter to the Romans had a political as well as theological impact.

Even twenty-first century theologians, pastors, priests, and Christians of all levels of biblical understanding use the name and teachings of Paul as a source of authority for Christian dogma. It is even often assumed that a listener is already quite familiar with the story behind this early Christian convert.

In order to find his mission work, Paul prayed without ceasing and had a direct experience with God the Creator. He followed this with prayer and meditation. It was through meditation, the quiet time when we listen to God whether while practicing yoga or just sitting or laying still without a barrage of acoustical noise and entertainment so common in today's world, that Paul was able to receive *the instruction* God gave him during his life. He had to listen for it. We must all take the time to listen to what God is saying to us.

What he found from listening to the instructions received during the quiet time of meditation was that what was needed within this framework of the newly forming Christian movement (and today) are groups in fellowship with one another but without tedious rules. "No meat on Friday" and "no dancing" are examples of these harsh rules that don't serve the needs of followers. We need to be sharing our purpose in our relationship with God with others without judgment; open to all with accepting other people's purpose, sharing with them our experience as God the Creator directs all of us in living the purpose he has created for us in this world. Forcing rules because of others' lifestyle or current understanding misses the mark of the teachings of Jesus.

After we see Jesus in scripture in the synagogue teaching the rabbis and doctors, his companions of choice are primarily those who chose to learn. He had no requirement for style of dress, education, profession, or level of awareness. He welcomed all. And his instruction was always to not judge. "If any one of you is without sin, let him be the first to throw a stone" (John 8:6–8) is a passage quoted by Christians and non-Christians, and during the first century AD, it was certainly a different way to behave. At that time, as today, devout Jews submitted to 613 laws.

It seems that Jesus and Paul both found that *too much rigidity in an already difficult life, as it was during that era on Earth, took away from the possibility of having a personal relationship with the Father.* And it began by first examining one's own role and place on his or her spiritual journey and then working toward uniting a community. Paul's reason for the church was to gather together to share knowledge. Churches with different answers may help us understand each other, but we may also have misunderstandings. I suggest here that we work together to try to learn about others and not judge. If we know where another is coming from, where he or she is on their personal journey toward God, then we can find a closer relationship with God through gaining a greater understanding of his children. Paul's teachings on this are included in the passage below.

Divisions in the Church

> 10 *I appeal to you, brothers, in the name of our Lord Jesus Christ, that all of you agree with one another so that there may be no divisions among you and that you may be perfectly united in mind and thought.*

> 11 *My brothers, some from Chloe's household have informed me that there are quarrels among you.*

> 12 *What I mean is this: One of you says, "I follow Paul"; another, "I follow Apollos"; another, "I follow Cephas"; still another, "I follow Christ."*

13 *Is Christ divided? Was Paul crucified for you? Were you baptized into the name of Paul?*

14 *I am thankful that I did not baptize any of you except Crispus and Gaius,*

15 *so no one can say that you were baptized into my name.*

16 *(Yes, I also baptized the household of Stephanas; beyond that, I don't remember if I baptized anyone else.)*

17 *For Christ did not send me to baptize, but to preach the gospel—not with words of human wisdom, lest the cross of Christ be emptied of its power.)*

–1 Corinthians

Paul seems to have had quite a sense of humor. Quick wit is necessary when dealing with anyone who is steadfast in his or her decision to be right in any area! Failing to see that we may indeed need to open up our own minds to the possibility that there may be another way to find God such as that Joe's path may not be the same path for Sam, and Joan and Sally are doing quite well being vegetarian Baptists doing yoga on Friday mornings. Your Catholic neighbor may indeed have a personal relationship with God despite your opinion of the rosary, and a Catholic's Protestant neighbor is not condemned for confessing directly to God versus in the confessional that serves him so well on his path. These and a host of other rules, I say, are what Paul spoke of in regard to "Christ divided."

It is important to understand that organized religion is man-made. But it can lead us to spirituality, and Paul directed us to stay with spirituality. We are to congregate. We often find support and faith from those around us. But our groups are to be inclusive, nonjudgmental, uplifting congregations of joy.

The word *sin* in Greek means to miss the mark. To miss the mark is sin. In other words, true sin, in its original form, was to lack understanding and fail to accomplish or "get it right." And the golden rule in Christian thought is to "do unto others as you would have done unto you." It all starts with loving God with all your heart and loving your neighbor as yourself, even when your neighbor (or family or friends) has a completely different concept and application of morality and ethics.

> *Today I will find the mission for my life. It will include extending my circle to those in need and to those whose path I may not recognize. Today I will learn what God truly wants for me, and I will release my desire to label others as good or bad by the rigidity set before us by the trappings of religion. Today I seek spirituality and God.*

[6]They were using this question as a trap, in order to have a basis for accusing him.

But Jesus bent down and started to write on the ground with his finger. [7] When they kept on questioning him, he straightened up and said to them, "If any one of you is without sin, let him be the first to throw a stone at her." [8]Again he stooped down and wrote on the ground.

–John 8:6–8 (New International Version)

CHAPTER 7

EARLY CHRISTIANS, EARLY SCIENCE, AND ANCIENT PHILOSOPHIES

Every decision you make is not a decision about what to do, it is a decision about who you are. When you see this and understand it, everything changes. You begin to see life in a new way. All events, occurrences, and situations turn into opportunities to do what you came here to do.

–Neal Donald Walsh, author of *Conversations with God*

Time magazine facilitated a debate recently on science versus religion between two scientists in an issue dated November 5, 2006, one the staunch atheist Richard Dawkins, "who occupies the Charles Simonyi professorship for the public understanding of science at Oxford University and author of *The God Delusion,* a book described in the article as a "rare volume whose position is so clear it forgoes a subtitle," and the other a convert from atheism, Francis Collins, who now combines a Christian understanding of God with a "devotion to genetics [which] is, if possible, greater than Dawkins's. Director of the national Human Genome Research Institute since 1993, Collins headed a multinational 2,400-scientist team that co-mapped the three billion biochemical letters of our genetic blueprint." As with many religious debates, it quickly deteriorated and stopped just short of name calling. Luckily for Christians, it wasn't Collins doing the name calling.

Collins explains the early Christian and early scientific understanding of the book of Genesis, which is often lost on many contemporary groups who fear the merging of faith and science. Some believers interpret Genesis 1 and 2 in a very literal way that is inconsistent, frankly, with our knowledge of the universe's age or of how living organisms are related to each other. St. Augustine [who lived during the fourth and fifth centuries AD] wrote that basically it is not possible to understand what was being described in Genesis. It was not intended as a science textbook. It was intended as a description about who God is, who we are, and what our relationship is supposed to be with God.

Augustine explicitly warns against a very narrow perspective that will put our faith at risk of looking ridiculous. If you step back from that one narrow interpretation, what the Bible describes is very consistent with the Big Bang.

It is important, also, to understand that early Christians received their basic understanding of the cosmology from the Jews, but took the books, translated into Greek and considered the Septuagint without the years of knowledge and study that formally educated Jews had via "Oral Torah," which was indeed compiled over a thousand years between the time of Moses ca. 1,200 BC and the compilation of the Torah into written documents, loosely the Christian Old Testament, around 250 BC. By the time of the writing of the Torah in the second century BC, there were vast commentaries on the books *not* contained in the translated texts turned over to the library in Alexandria, Egypt, from where the Christians obtained the scholarly copies.

So what did the Jews believe about the creation of the world and the entire universe when Jesus was born as a Jew in the first century AD? If we remind ourselves that Jesus is reported to have visited and taught the rabbis and doctors (one and the same during his time), he obviously was educated not only in the writings in Torah, but also the hundreds of years of commentaries from rabbis who had gone before. But it wasn't until the Middle Ages that a Jewish theologian shared these concepts with the Western world. Jews did not invite outsiders to join them. One was born into the "chosen people," not invited in.

One of the issues I see as a problem causing the decline in participation in many of the world's great religious denominations is that some movements have failed to reconcile scripture and its understanding with the revelations of science. Both Christians and Jews were aware of this phenomenon in the early part of our era, but those who were able to understand the concepts were educated and few. The masses did not have the mental capacity to grasp the concept, or the leaders of the day thought so; therefore, people were kept in the dark on these issues.

The insistence on reading Genesis, for example, as a timeline of history has been shown to be a failure to get the message of the Bible itself. It misses the mark, showing how religious beliefs and the teachings of Christian followers of Christ will begin to show how it is humans who have corrupted the message. One need not separate religion from science. In fact, Jesus was born into a world that had a very Greek understanding of the universe and how it came into existence. Many contemporary beliefs about the nature of the soul do not come from Judaism and the scriptures passed down via the Septuagint, but from Greek philosophers and scholars such as Plato and Aristotle. Jesus, having been an educated Jewish man living in the world's center of intellectual thought, Egypt, in his early childhood, would have been very familiar with these works and clearly his departure from traditional Jewish views on many subject show the influence of his education on his three-year mission and the teachings. Scholars argue that he very likely spoke Greek, and many New Testament books have early versions composed or at least translated into the educated language of the day—Greek.

Jesus spoke in parables, he used analogies like the Greek Philosophers, and he taught a radical concept of "love thy neighbor" versus the standard "eye for an eye" treatment of others by most of his contemporaries and the rejection of outsiders commonly practiced by many ethnic and religious groups of his time. So what did Plato teach about the creation of the earth and the human experience?

The core of modern cosmology, or the understanding of the universe and how it was formed, grew out of ancient Greek thought, later adopted by the Christian Church. The underlying theme in Greek science is the use of observation and experimentation to search for simple, universal laws. This struggle led to the development of the biggest philosophical achievement of humankind, the philosophy of science. Indirectly, through an examination of our myths and creation stories, we developed the ideas and techniques that later would become the basis for the sciences of today. But it took many years and underwent much evolution to arrive at our more enlightened state we have now for the world around us. Central to the Greek understanding of the natural world, cosmology is the belief that the order of the universe can be expressed in mathematical principles. In a nutshell, this means that despite the chaos we seem to live amidst, there is an established order.

Observation and contemplation of the physical world and its phenomenal events led Plato to hypothesize that there were two universes: the physical world and a nonmaterial world of "forms," perfect aspects of everyday things such as a table, a chair, a bird, and ideas and emotions, joy, sadness, even action. One might call this a parallel universe. Plato argued in his *Allegory of the Cave,* that the objects *and ideas* in our material world are "shadows" of the forms. He suggests that our physical world is not really solid. Science, via the field of quantum physics, which is the study of subatomic particles, supports this in super law 1: The Law of Perpetual Transmutation of Energy.

Everything is energy. Energy is motion. Energy never stands still. It takes one form then another. Change is all there is. And because we understand that everything is made up of molecules, made up of atoms, which are basically energy and mostly empty, then Plato almost got it right! Add to Plato's forms a more contemporary understanding known as super law 2: The Law of Vibration, which states that *thought* is one of the most powerful and potent forms of energy vibrating at one of the highest frequencies, then Plato's concept of ideas existing in this physical realm and the other universe is also a brilliant understanding for his time.

The concept of an "anthropocentric" universe refers to "man centered." This may seem amusing and arrogant to think we are indeed the center of the universe, but it was the understanding of pre-Christian and Christian humans that we are indeed the most important beings on Earth and in the universe, ergo, in the center of God's mind. Think of the derogatory statements made about people who may seem to be a bit too egotistical, such as, "He/she thinks the world revolves around him/her." It implies we know that the earth is indeed in orbit and not even the solar system!

Both Plato and Pythagoras influenced the first logically consistent cosmological worldview, developed by the Greeks in the fourth century BC. This early cosmology was an expansion of the Greek theory of matter proposed by Empedocles. This theory states that all matter in the universe is composed of some combination of four elements: earth, water, fire, and air. These four elements arise from the working of the two properties of hotness (and its contrary coldness) and dryness (and its contrary wetness) upon an original unqualified or primitive matter. The possible combinations of these two properties of primitive matter give rise to the four elements, or elemental forms.

Though our modern understanding of the universal elements is far greater, as we have an ever-increasing periodic table of elements, the world of science continues to explore our world, but this ancient understanding of the universe leads us to super law 3: The Law of Relativity. Everything in our material world is made real by its relationship to something else (i.e., hot only exists because we compare it to cold). Relationships are everything, and everything is due to relationships with other things. The ancient scientific understanding of the universe is still quite helpful.

Going back to the Platonic cosmology, elements had a natural tendency to separate in space, which is true: fire moved outward, away from the earth, and earth moved inward, with air and water being intermediate. Thus, each of these five elements occupied a unique place in the heavens (earth elements were heavy and, therefore, low; fire elements were light and located up high). Thus, Plato's system also became one of the first cosmological models.

By going back through history to early Christian thought on the creation of the world and the understanding of the message of Genesis and how it has developed into what we have today, I hope to show that belief in its inherit "truth" need not be an issue. Humans have struggled to understand how we got here and what we're here for throughout time. And on a metaphorical level, it isn't contradictory to believe its message, for as you can see, the message is there. There is a God, and he created the universe. To try to discount his role in science is lame. What we need is a greater understanding and a willingness to arrive finally at the conclusion that we don't now, nor will we ever, know it all.

The Holy Scriptures Are Our Letters from Home

God is not what you imagine or what you think you understand. If you understand you have failed. —St. Augustine

> [1] *In the beginning God created the heavens and the earth.*
>
> **–Genesis 1**

> [1] *Thus the heavens and the earth were completed in all their vast array.*
>
> [2] *By the seventh day God had finished the work he had been doing; so on the seventh day he rested from all his work.* [3] *And God blessed the seventh day and made it holy, because on it he rested from all the work of creating that he had done.*
>
> **–Genesis 2**

CHAPTER 8

MARTIN LUTHER: THE MONK WHO CHANGED THE CHRISTIAN CONCEPT

> *When we are truly perfect, we pretend not to be. God creates us perfect. We need to accept our perfection as individuals—God's children.*
>
> **–Author unknown**

Martin Luther shook the world when he took on the power of the Catholic Church in 1517 and exposed the citizens of Christendom to an opportunity to engage in a struggle for a personal relationship, for all Christians not just clergy, with God. The onset of the Enlightenment, an era that was ushered in with the then recent invention and use of the Gutenberg press, the printing machine that allowed Luther's ideas and philosophies to rage across Europe, saw radical changes first within the frame of the religious institution of the early sixteenth century. How did Luther and other reformers of his time bring a new awareness of the Christian message and how it affects the quality of life on Earth? Luther's effectiveness in this area was recognized, though as damaging, by the church hierarchy. He'd unleashed a change, a radical departure from the ways of total control of the populace, which could never be undone. And we know from history that essential things only happen when there is a need. The timing was right for Luther's ideas; therefore, his "new way" of thinking spread because humans were ready to receive the information.

Luther left a number of written works, as he seemed to have somewhat of an obsessive-compulsive personality. His 95 Theses, in fact, were all reasons why indulgences were wrong. Any of us, given the task, could probably find 10 or 20, but 95? Plenary indulgences were "pardons" sold by the church of his time in order to obtain forgiveness for sin. These indulgences promised escape from Purgatory to the bearer for a fee, but could also be purchased to pardon the sins of the deceased. The potential income of this fund-raising expedition was astronomical, and the proceeds were to fund the building of the elaborate St. Peter's Basilica in Rome.

I think it is important to realize here, too, that St. Peter's is not the seat of the papacy; the pope is the Bishop of Rome, and that seat is located in St. John in Lateran's Basilica, which is still the case today. St. Peter's is, however, located within the Vatican. So many Europeans of Luther's day saw this architectural mission as a great and unnecessary extravagance by the pope. But this was not the first time Luther found fault with the superfluous expenditures of the church in Rome. However, it was the "need" he saw that caused him to post his famous 95 Theses on the church door in Wittenberg on October 31, 1517. This action was typical for engaging any scholar in debate; most scholars and scientists at that time were clergy, but not all.

Luther was directly challenging the papal representative in town, Johann Tetzel, to a debate, but the Dominican Friar Tetzel would not engage Luther, and instead sent the document to Rome, causing scandal and the very real threat of Luther's excommunication and execution by the Inquisition as a heretic. A contemporary of Luther's, Philip Melancthon, wrote and published the life of Luther, titled *A History of the Life and Actions of the Very Reverend Dr. Martin Luther*, in 1549. Melancthon gives us more insight into Luther by looking at his entire life from early childhood. Luther was not simply a priest. He was a highly educated and passionate man. Melancthon tells us that as a student and novice monk

> *[Luther's] spirit thus thirsting for knowledge, continually sought a more abundant and better supply. He read many of the works of the ancient Latin authors, as Cicero, Virgil, Livy, and others; these he perused, not as schoolboys commonly do, merely by gathering together a vocabulary of words, but for solid instruction, and as mirrors of human life, by which means he gained a full perception of the views and opinions of these writers, and as his memory was both accurate and tenacious, much of what he read and heard was clearly placed before his mental vision. Hence it was remarkable that even in his youth, the talents of Luther were the admiration of the whole University.*

Luther did not simply study and learn about all things he could both spiritually and temporally. He actually examined his beliefs and the order of the natural world. He put his faith into practice, often to the extreme, in order to truly learn about the nature of God and the world. His entrance into the monastery, a particularly rigid group with extreme practices of a life of rigor, and often corporal mortification, to purge one of one's sins was one of self-examination and torturous practices to attempt to achieve piety.

Luther struggled to find the personal relationship with God now available to all Christians but then denied to just about everyone. You believed what the Church told you to believe or you were considered a heretic. Catholicism has evolved since, but this was indeed a medieval mind-set with limited understanding of many things. There was only one way to be a Christian, and this included a list of sacraments and rituals that were added by generations of church authorities. Luther could only find two: baptism and communion.

Luther labeled this concept *sola fideles*, Latin for "faith alone." To this Luther added the idea of *sola scriptora*, or "scripture alone." These two ideas, not the list of sacraments and rituals performed by the clergy, was what led to salvation. The personal faith of the individual and the information obtained in scriptures, canonical scripture, not the additional texts considered tradition in the church, was all that was to be considered necessary for anyone to reach heaven. In fact, Luther's expertise as a biblical scholar led him to reexamine the documents in some Bibles called most commonly "The Apocrypha" and remove it as scripture. Catholic Bibles still contain these texts considered "Deutero-canonical Texts."

The problem with these documents, Luther and others point out, is that the Jews did not consider them historically accurate as early as the first century AD. They were included in the Septuagint, the Jewish text translated to Greek, which early Christians used, but there could easily be found in each of the works historical inaccuracies. Also, Jews rejected any "books" included in the Septuagint that were not available in an original Hebrew format. In other words, Jews very early on considered these texts forgeries. Luther was adept in many languages; therefore, he was able to explore many avenues of thought. At this time, all scholarly and scientific writing was done in Latin, Greek, or Arabic in the Western world. He was a well-respected scholar and theologian.

It is usually the case that it takes a radical figure to change the way humans think, especially for the better! But with most changes in our world, whether personal or on a public or global scale, change is rarely met with enthusiasm. Even great preachers of peace movements such as Mohandas Gandhi radically shook thinking and made enemies for their teachings of nonviolence! The Reverend Dr. Martin Luther King, Jr., who used Gandhi's teachings of nonviolent resistance, met with a tragic death by assassination for his stands on civil rights in the United States. These figures who change our way of thinking and being are often men or women who have also experienced "the dark night of the soul."

Luther's writings explored the early teachings of the Christian movement where he felt the true teachings lay—the fundamental truths, so to speak. The actions taken by this man, friend to many, and enemy to even more, gave Christians the ability to pursue their own spiritual path, and thereby more effectively initiate a better life for themselves. When we are on a path with God, a personal daily journey for living life to the fullest, we can create the life of happiness, health, and wealth that is our birthright and what the Father wants for us. Luther says it well with his personal prayer: "Establish in us O God! That which Thou hast wrought, and perfect the work which Thou hast begun in us to Thy glory, Amen."

A recent sermon by Robert Anthony Schuller told a story about a large boat in a storm related to the scriptural story of the storm on the lake of Galilee that Christ calmed. There was a large sailing boat on the lake. The sailors were up to the task to work the boat through the storm until they heard a strange noise striking one side of the boat then another with enough force to create a hole if the cannon could not be tied down. They sent a team of men to retie the cannon and protect the boat inside. Schuller used this metaphor to relate how most of us are strong without and in control until the storm begins within. You must have faith in God to deal with the storm within. Shifting times and undependable emotions can tear us apart. Certainly none of us have faced an external enemy the size of the one faced by Martin Luther. Remember to remain enthusiastic. Acknowledging God within us, he is able to fill the void. This source is indefatigable.

> [34]Then Peter began to speak: "I now realize how true it is that God does not show favoritism [35]but accepts men from every nation who fear him and do what is right. [36]You know the message God sent to the people of Israel, telling the good news of peace through Jesus Christ, who is Lord of all.
>
> **–Acts 10:34–36 (New International Version)**

CHAPTER 9

I THINK THEREFORE I AM

When you judge another, you do not define them. You define yourself.

–Wayne Dyer

Rene Descartes was a famous French mathematician, scientist, and philosopher who lived about fifty years after Martin Luther. Descartes lived in the rapidly changing Europe that Luther helped to usher in as countless other reformers took action in the new freedom and protection they had from local rulers who decided to allow them to preach and teach their messages of reform and a return to what many taught were more pure beliefs. Descartes was arguably the first major philosopher in the modern era to make a serious effort to defeat skepticism. His views about knowledge and certainty, as well as his views about the relationship between mind and body, have been very influential over the last three centuries.

Born in the late sixteenth century, Descartes recognized that he thought. Thought creates change. He existed, and the only proof of his existence was "I think, therefore, I am." This is a powerful yet simple argument. According to Descartes, "I am" means being, and "I think" means change. Change is necessary for the awareness of one's existence. What we see with Descartes is a merging in one man's philosophies and a well-respected man in all of his fields of religion, spirituality, and science. It's like the swing of a pendulum, where science will prove something and then try to disprove its previous religious understanding. But I see a new awareness coming where spirituality can and will embrace scientific discoveries and come to appreciate how this greater understanding will then increase faith. In fact, the new field of science, specifically quantum physics, shows us that thought is not only energy but the highest form of energy!

Descartes's efforts to combine religion and science have continued into the last century, when scientists and theologians began their greatest joining together, in my opinion. People who want to know God and how he works and designed the universe desire to study the natural word via science, which includes our world rules or laws, including gravity, the seven laws of quantum physics, and the extension to giving, gratitude, accountability, partnerships, vision, paradigms, and understanding. This is the power that is available to all of us. I believe this can be documented in scripture. It's been done. It is being done. And it is in no way heretical or false teaching. We need only open up our minds and use our God-given abilities to interpret rather than react and reject from lack of understanding or a need to be right at the expense of making others wrong.

And by striving to be our absolute best, we aspire to be more like God. Descartes "proved" God is perfect by comparing him to the imperfect human. Genesis says God made us in his own image, but as Descartes shows, that cannot be because we are by our very nature imperfect, striving for perfection. Descartes shows us that we know that perfection exists because we are imperfect. An attribute, which has great value for Descartes, is the veracity of God.

Accepting ourselves for being human is a great way to remain enthusiastic and ride the tide of events and people who flow into our lives. We cannot change another human being, but by the understanding of ourselves.

Rene Descartes actually used the Law of Relativity to describe some of his philosophy, though he never called it such. He used diametrically opposing ideas to get his point across, such as perfect and imperfect, mountain and valley, and cause and effect. Through these comparisons, he helped us to also see the relationship between infinite and spirit or god and matter. All of this relates to quantum physics and our more modern acceptance of God and man who accepts God as a co-creator.

The quantum field contains all knowledge. We are blessed by this, as was Paul. "Praying without ceasing" connects us with all knowledge. Psalm 46:10 states, "Be still and know that I am God," and it is God who brings understanding of all things, for he created us. He is source. He is the zero-point field. The originator. These are two scriptural passages that most of us know by heart. The concepts of quantum physics are not new to us. The way we understand and apply them is indeed changing. It's all there in holy scripture, as Luther contends. How we sift through it is changing as science continues to show us explanations of God's creations.

Descartes also wrestled with the concept of doubt. Doubt is simply a lack of faith, and when we doubt in the extreme, we then lack in faith. Lack of faith, or doubt, leads to fear. Some say fear is simply "false evidence appearing real." We must all doubt at some point because it gives us the basis of comparison we need as humans to grasp a concept fully. Without it, we cannot trust, but the struggle for us is to overcome the habitual doubt and trust, or have faith, more than we doubt. But on the flip side, our doubt becomes detrimental when we allow it to become fear.

If I decided to go on national television and argue for the existence of God, much of the American public would think I was a lunatic. But we expect such arguments from men (or women) of the cloth. But for Descartes, he lived in a world that to think otherwise, that God did not exist, would be the lunacy, not the way our society thinks today.

Descartes's ideas changed the way humans view themselves. It got us thinking. It forced us to explore even more ideas, more concepts, and more possibilities. It began to open us up to a better understanding of who we are and why we're here. We are on Earth to have an experience of the divine. We are here to see how we can best serve God by serving others.

[10] Be still, and know that I am God; I will be exalted among the nations, I will be exalted in the earth.

–Psalm 46:10 (New International Version)

CHAPTER 10

NICOLAUS COPERNICUS
RESTORING THE STARS:

> *Belief in the things you can see and touch is not belief at all, but to believe in the unseen is a triumph and a blessing.*
>
> **–Abraham Lincoln**

Throughout our history, Christians have looked to the church for answers, and as we've seen, not just the answers that apply to the condition of our soul and our chances at salvation. For most of the past 2,000 years, the Christian church was the only source for education at all! Included in that were all of the emerging fields of science.

Nicolaus Copernicus lived from AD 1473–1543. He was a mathematician and astronomer who proposed that the sun was stationary in the center of the universe and the earth revolved around it. This was heretical. It is that simple. It contradicted what the Bible says regarding the formation of the earth and the cosmos in the book of Genesis. Heresy was punishable by death during Copernicus's life as the "Holy" Inquisition was in full force. One did not need to be a Jew or a practitioner of witchcraft to be targeted as an enemy of the church. Copernicus knew this and was a reluctant revolutionary.

Copernicus was highly disturbed by the failure of Ptolemy's geocentric model of the universe to follow Aristotle's requirement for the uniform circular motion of all celestial bodies and determined to eliminate Ptolemy's "equan," an imaginary point around which the bodies seemed to follow that requirement. He decided that he could achieve his goal only through a heliocentric model with the sun as the center. He thereby created a concept of a universe in which the distances of the planets from the sun bore a direct relationship to the size of their orbits. At the time, Copernicus's heliocentric idea was very controversial; nevertheless, it was the start of a change in the way the world was viewed, and Copernicus came to be seen as the initiator of the Scientific Revolution.

This heliocentric system was proposed by Copernicus in a book called *On the Revolutions of the Heavenly Bodies* very near the end of his life. The ordering of the planets known to Copernicus in this new system is illustrated in the following description, which we recognize as the modern and correct ordering of those planets.

This ordering depicts the earth as just another planet and the third from the sun. The moon is in orbit around the earth, not the sun. The stars are distant objects that do not revolve around the sun. Instead, the earth is assumed to rotate once in twenty-four hours, causing the stars to appear to revolve around the earth in the opposite direction.

Copernicus published his heretical idea. Earth is not a special place. Imagine the implications here! Earth is not special? How can that be if we are the children of an omnipotent and omniscient Almighty? Aren't we the center of his attention? His *only* focus?

Genesis 1:14 states:

> 14 *And God said, "Let there be lights in the expanse of the sky to separate the day from the night, and let them serve as signs to mark seasons and days and years,*
>
> 15 *and let them be lights in the expanse of the sky to give light on the earth." And it was so.*
>
> 16 *God made two great lights—the greater light to govern the day and the lesser light to govern the night. He also made the stars.*
>
> 17 *God set them in the expanse of the sky to give light on the earth,*
>
> 18 *to govern the day and the night, and to separate light from darkness. And God saw that it was good.*
>
> 19 *And there was evening, and there was morning—the fourth day.*

According to Copernicus, our solar system had a sun at the center with planets in orbit in perfect circles upon circles. He emphasized the busyness of place. The lights in the sky were not there to serve the earth. The earth revolved around the sun. It's backward to the accepted thought of the day. And what does that mean spiritually and religiously if the authoritative book and the authorities were wrong about where we exist in the universe? Does that mean that they were also wrong about God himself?

These are and were questions that stood to rattle the populace, and keeping this sort of information from the public was considered crucial. And it was taken quite seriously. But the church was finding that, due to the rapidly increasing ease of transmitting new ideas via the written word produced on the Gutenberg press, the effort proved futile.

Copernicus was an unlikely and an unwilling heretical instigator for this challenging reordering of the solar system. It is believed that his book was only published at the end of his life because he feared ridicule and disfavor by his peers and by the church, which had elevated the ideas of Aristotle to the level of religious dogma. This reluctant revolutionary, however, set a chain of events in motion that would eventually produce one of the greatest revolutions in thinking that Western civilization has ever seen. His ideas remained rather obscure for about 100 years after his death. But, in the seventeenth century, the work of Kepler, Galileo, and Newton would build on the heliocentric Copernican universe and produce the change in thinking that would sweep away completely the ideas of Aristotle as truth and replace them with the modern view of astronomy and natural science. This sequence of events is commonly called the *Copernican Revolution*.

Another scientist, Johannes Kepler, in 1610, working with astronomer Tychoe Bryed, described mathematically how the planets orbit the sun, but not why. He explained that we exist in a sun-centered universe, in which the orbits appear to be elliptical, and now with mathematical formulas, the ideas were becoming more explicable and beginning to make more sense. Unfortunately for Christians, a dichotomy still exists between what happens in the heavens and what happens on Earth, and the likelihood that God exists as was taught for centuries began to be questioned more and more. If Genesis is not "true," then what else in the Holy Bible was simply a fabricated story? Was the story of Noah and the Flood true? Was Moses really the leader extraordinaire called by God? And it did not stop there.

The beginning of the Scientific Revolution caused widespread questioning of all education. Who was the authority and on which topics? What else would science prove? Is science then of God because we are taught that all things are of God? And during Copernicus's time, many Protestant groups were emerging that took a more fundamental approach to the indisputable validity to all aspects of the Bible.

Many times our subconscious beliefs hold us back. We tend to store information fed to us as children in our subconscious minds, so we take as "gospel" all information told to us in story form, whether biblical stories or fairy tales. But we kept them in our subconscious, and they then tend to block us in moving forward. Is this how Satan works? Indeed, in the first 12 years of life, we knew that God is love.

In Matthew 18:3, Jesus said, "I tell you the truth, unless you change and become like little children, you will never enter the kingdom of heaven." We must learn to be open to new ideas like we were when we were children, when we could learn new concepts without the baggage of our subconscious programming and beliefs.

As we pass into puberty, however, and begin our own lives, not those directed by teachers, ministers, friends, parents, uncles, aunts, and grandparents (and often the older the authoritarian, the more "right" they seemed), some of the beliefs they passed on to us would not help to carry us forward into life very well. At least not with the mission God has for our lives.

It is necessary for us to find a way to change those beliefs that prevent us from moving forward, growing, and becoming the servants of God he intends us to be. As co-creators of our lives, we must rid ourselves of beliefs that we grew up with that created the filter for what we are able to see and what we are able to do just as early modern era Christians had to do with the new scientific evidence provided to them by men such as Copernicus. It was a challenge to their entire belief system, but it proved more enlightening to see that indeed it was so.

The best way to eradicate these negative beliefs of our upbringing and programming in our young and later adult life is to ask our spirit within the unconscious mind, which controls our habits, to change and to enable us with enthusiasm (God within) to be able to move forward easily in order to achieve God's mission in our lives. Our lives are in constant change, and we've been informed of this for centuries. In the Old Testament book of Daniel 2, verse 21, we read:

> *He changes times and seasons;*
> *he sets up kings and deposes them.*
> *He gives wisdom to the wise*
> *and knowledge to the discerning.*

When we change our inner beliefs, we are able to change our outer reality, and this is done in accordance with God's plan for which he gives us signs and signals if we are spiritually fit. And in doing so, we change God's world to be more fully aware. We can see his greatness with more clarity. Our personal belief in what we are doing is the key to success. We must speak from our heart.

It is much the same today as we go further and further with science, especially quantum physics, to understand that it is our thinking that is limited. Do you really believe God is omnipotent and omnipresent? If you do, then why would he limit anything for us? If he is truly among us, then aren't all things possible? And would such a powerful being limit the potential of his creation? Each of us is endowed with God-given abilities and talents, and it is in his honor to bring them forward for the good of all humans and the earth itself.

Raymond Holliwell, author of *Working with the Law,* contends that the law of God denies man nothing. He states that God intends each of us to succeed and become great. We are limitless beings endowed with a wonderful set of faculties to insure success. There are no resources or goals out of our reach as our purpose is to succeed in every area. By understanding the principles and laws that work with nature and using them in the way God intends, we are able to fulfill every dream and make every possibility a reality.

We were not given the gifts we have to waste them. We were put here to use them to the glory of God, and God wants each of his children to be happy, healthy, and prosperous. He placed great people in history in order to initiate the evolution of thinking so that we arrived here in the twenty-first century with a greater understanding of what our purpose is and with the thinking ability to accept the progress of science yet still hold fast to faith. We can reconcile "lame science and blind religion" into a greater understanding and awareness. We can progress scientifically while at the same time realizing that we have a mission as humans to recognize the spiritual nature of the natural world and everyone and everything in it.

[14] *And God said, "Let there be lights in the expanse of the sky to separate the day from the night, and let them serve as signs to mark seasons and days and years, [15] and let them be lights in the expanse of the sky to give light on the earth." And it was so. [16] God made two great lights— the greater light to govern the day and the lesser light to govern the night. He also made the stars. [17] God set them in the expanse of the sky to give light on the earth, [18] to govern the day and the night, and to separate light from darkness. And God saw that it was good. [19] And there was evening, and there was morning—the fourth day.*

–Genesis 1:14–19 (New International Version)

[3]Jesus reached out his hand and touched the man. "I am willing," he said. "Be clean!" Immediately he was cured[a] of his leprosy.

–Matthew 8:3 (New International Version)

CHAPTER 11

SIR ISAAC NEWTON: FALLING APPLES

> *Whatever you can do or dream, you can begin it.*
> *Boldness has genius, power, and magic in it.*
>
> **–Goethe**

English physicist, mathematician, astronomer, natural philosopher, alchemist, and theologian, Sir Isaac Newton lived to be age 84. Born on January 4, 1643, his mother was widowed prior to his birth, and she left to marry an elderly clergyman when Newton was only 3. His grandparents raised him until the age of 11, when his mother returned after the death of her second husband. Plans were for him to take over the family farm when he reached 18, but this proved to be a failure for the farm and a huge blessing for the advancement of science in the Western world.

His maternal uncle, also a clergyman who had studied at Cambridge, persuaded his mother that it would be better for Isaac to go to university, so in 1661, he went to Trinity College, Cambridge. Isaac paid his way through college for the first three years by waiting tables and cleaning rooms. In 1664, he was elected a scholar, guaranteeing four years of financial support. Unfortunately, at that time the plague was spreading across Europe and reached Cambridge in the summer of 1665. The university closed, and Newton returned home, where he spent two years concentrating on problems in mathematics and physics. Interestingly, one of the major life events that saw Martin Luther commit to a life of study was also the bubonic plague that raged across Europe nearly every decade for centuries.

Newton later wrote that it was during this time that he first understood the theory of gravitation and the theory of optics. He was the first to realize that white light is made up of the colors of the rainbow, and he was the first to have a broad understanding of mathematics, both integral and differential calculus and infinite series. However, he was always reluctant to publish anything, at least until it appeared that someone else might get credit for what he had found earlier. So we have here yet another reluctant scientific revolutionist!

Sir Isaac Newton's first major *public* scientific achievement was the invention, design, and construction of a reflecting telescope. He ground the mirror, built the tube, and even made his own tools for the job. This was a real advance in telescope technology, and it ensured his election to membership in the Royal Society. The mirror gave a sharper image than was possible with a large lens because a lens focuses different colors at slightly different distances, an effect called *chromatic aberration*.

Projectiles and Planets

What Newton is most famous for is the central topic of his work *Principia,* which explains the universality of the gravitational force, or simply put, gravity. This is surely a universal principle we all accept as "truth" though explicable only scientifically. There is a widely accepted legend that Newton saw an apple fall in his garden and thought of it in terms of an attractive gravitational force toward the earth. He realized the same force might extend as far as the moon. Newton was familiar with Galileo's work on projectiles, and he proposed that the moon's motion in orbit could be understood as a natural extension of that theory.

Later in the 1670s, Newton became very interested in theology. He studied Hebrew scholarship and ancient and modern theologians at great length. Newton became convinced that Christianity had departed from the original teachings of Christ as was already being proposed by Christian reformers throughout Europe. He felt unable to accept the beliefs of the Church of England (Episcopalian in the United States), which was unfortunate because he was required as a fellow of Trinity College to take holy orders. There was not, at that time, a large doctrinal difference between the Roman Catholic Church and the Church of England because the major difference lay in the simple lack of recognition by the Church of England of the papacy in Rome. Happily, the Church of England was more flexible than Galileo had found the Catholic Church in these matters, and King Charles II issued a royal decree excusing Newton from the necessity of taking holy orders! Actually, to prevent this being a wide precedent, the decree specified that, in perpetuity, the Lucasian professor need not take holy orders.

I think it is important to note that Newton, too, was a religious man and a scientist whose problem with religion lay not in its lack of willingness to embrace scientific principles, but that it strayed from the teachings of the founder. He could see that the current state of theology in his time was simply lacking in understanding of the original message. Religion became too caught up in doctrine and dogma and less focused on the concepts presented that brought one into a closer relationship with God.

Sir Isaac Newton furthered the understanding of the natural world and the order of the cosmos, thus advancing the scientific revolution begun by the reluctant Copernicus. We will see that many scientists have done this. They expand upon and improve the ideas and explanations of those who went before. It often produces extreme discomfort for those who become attached to any explanation as being the ultimate truth.

German philosopher Hegel proposed the idea that all social and scientific change is explained dialectically. We begin with an issue or a thesis. In order to challenge this accepted idea, we are often confronted with its extreme opposite or challenge. He refers to this as the "antithesis." This "pendulum swing," however, usually comes back to an improved understanding or growth. This he labels "synthesis." And because we are always changing and growing, Hegel's dialectic argument is perfect because the synthesis inevitably becomes the thesis point as we gain greater understanding.

As I said earlier, Newton is most famous for his acknowledgment of the Law of Gravity. He said, "This law also takes place in attractions." This of course is central to Newton's (and our) view of the universe. If the earth is attracting the moon gravitationally with a certain force holding it in its orbit, then the moon is attracting the earth with an equal force. So why isn't the earth going around the moon? The answer is that the masses are so different. The earth's mass is more than 100 times that of the moon.

Newton's Third Law: Action and Reaction

Having established that a force—the action of another body—was necessary to cause a body to change its state of motion, Newton made one further crucial observation: such forces *always* arise as a *mutual interaction* of two bodies, and the other body also feels the force, but in the opposite direction.

Law 3: **To every action there is always opposed an equal and opposite reaction:** *or the mutual actions of two bodies upon each other are always equal, and directed to contrary parts.*

Like Copernicus, Newton seemed to understand that his purpose was to show the world something great yet maintain his humble nature. According to Fred Allen Wolfe, author of *Taking the Quantum Leap: The New Physics for Non-Scientists*, Newton spoke of his own role in life as such:

"I do not know what I may appear to the world; but to my self I seem to have been only a boy playing on the seashore and directing myself in now and then finding a smoother pebble or a prettier shell than ordinary, whilst the great ocean of truth lay all undiscovered before me."

The concept of *cause and effect* came through Newton. The future became a consequence of the past. Our thoughts, according to Newton, were explained by "Newton's machine." This is usually referred to as "the watchmaker" analogy. The hand of God set the machine in motion, and no one could stop it. Nothing was left to chance. This view is known as *determinism*. Everything is already determined by God. I think it discounts the idea of free will or free agency. We all have choices, and I believe God leaves our decisions up to us. Though I do appreciate Newton's radical changes in thinking and his explanations of the universal law of gravity and others, assuming God has already determined every aspect of our lives takes away the joys and sorrows of life—both of which are necessary for our own personal growth. If not for free will, we would not be able to learn from our choices. We decided the "why, where, and when" but not the "what." For it is the "what" in our lives that is God's mission for us, toward which we should be using our free will.

Newton first called gravity a distant force. No cosmic strings—yet powerful was the influence of this never-observed yet totally present phenomenon and cause of acceleration.

The ideas of determinism and no-free-will physics were able to explain a remarkably large number of physical phenomena from the movement of the planets to the kinetic motions of tiny particles within a closed volume of gas with only a few principles. It became the model of human knowledge.

So what does this mean for us in our lives? We do have free will. God has and is governing every aspect of our lives by universal laws. Gravity is an easy one to understand. God assures us often that if we continue to ignore the truth of the universal laws, we will continue to achieve the same unproductive results in our lives. However, if we become willing to change and to flow with the changes that occur, understanding they are indeed all part of God's world, we will find it much easier to proceed with life, and a life of abundance and prosperity, because we are working *with God* versus against him. If you don't believe me, see how often you can drop a pen and not have it hit the ground.

[32]Then you will know the truth, and the truth will set you free.

–John 8:32 (New International Version)

[25]But the man who looks intently into the perfect law that gives freedom, and continues to do this, not forgetting what he has heard, but doing it—he will be blessed in what he does.

–James 1:25 (New International Version)

CHAPTER 12

GALILEO GALILEI

> *The secret to success is to work harder on yourself than you do on the job. That's good advice. If you work hard on the job, you will make a living. If you work hard on yourself, you will make a fortune.*
>
> **–Jim Rohn**

Galileo Galilei was yet another reluctant revolutionary thinker who lived in the sixteenth and seventeenth centuries. He was an Italian physicist, mathematician, astronomer, and philosopher who played a major role in the scientific revolution. His achievements include improvements to the telescope and consequent astronomical observations and support for Copernicanism. Galileo has been called the father of modern observational astronomy, the father of modern physics, the father of science, and the father of modern science. Yet throughout his life, he remained a devout Christian.

Galileo discovered active observation in the movement of the pendulum and a clock discovered in church—the first way to measure time. A pendulum can be relied upon to measure time. The movement, whether wide or narrow, remains the same movement. But Galileo was a visionary; he was able to see things others could not. We often cannot see something we cannot identify. We don't know what it is we're looking at, and the mind cannot process the information, so it rejects it.

There is a story of Galileo's experience with his inquisitors. These learned men were unable to see minute organisms when they looked into the microscope, the same creatures and the things that Galileo had been opened to, because they had nothing with which to compare them. John Assaraf tells us in his work on "How the Brain Works" (2009) that our nonconscious mind "looks for patterns and images in our 'outside world' that match our 'inside world'. Information that doesn't match up gets dropped." This is exactly what happened with the Inquisitors. They could not recognize something new; therefore, it did not exist.

This is similar to the story of the South American Aztec Indians who had no idea what they saw when the Spanish ships approached their shore the first time. They had never seen a ship before. It was not in their perception. They had nothing to compare it with. What all do we miss because it is not in our perception?

In Philippians 3:14–16, we are told:

> 14 *I press on toward the goal to win the prize for which*
> *God has called me heavenward in Christ Jesus.*

15 All of us who are mature should take such a view of things. And if on some point you think differently, that too God will make clear to you.

16 Only let us live up to what we have already attained.

According to Fred Allen Wolf in his book, *Taking the Quantum Leap: The New Physics for Non-Scientists,* Galileo also did an experiment in front of the di Medici family, demonstrating that things roll down hill at the same speed regardless of how much they weigh as opposed to Aristotle's theory many years before that things would roll down based on their weight. Aristotle thought that heavier objects would roll faster than lighter ones. Galileo's mind for analysis meant the simplification and discovery of God's laws. By reaching out and touching the universe, Galileo set the precedent of modern experimental physics.

Galileo did experiments. He not only observed the natural world around him, but he tested it. What is the natural state of motion on Earth? He also did some observational astronomy, and this was made easier as he developed a telescope in which he saw three things that shook the foundations of the beliefs about the universe. The first was that the planet Jupiter had four little dots lined up on the side that change positions. These were referred to as Galilean satellites of Jupiter. He saw them as a miniature solar system. This helped to confirm the notion that nothing is special about Earth, though we know that not to be the case now, but it did show that other planets have moons like the earth's.

The second thing Galileo noted was the "Phases of Venus." When Venus is full, it appears to us as a very small circle. Also, when it's full, it's farthest away, but when it's a crescent, it appears much bigger. Again this verifies the Copernican idea of Earth not being a special planet, per se, in the solar system.

Sunspots, or dark blemishes on the surface of the sun, showed Galileo that the celestial realm is not perfect. Why should it obey some perfect laws? This idea established a non-perfect heaven that would destroy some of the basic teachings of the church! What then did Christians have to look forward to in the hereafter if heaven itself was not perfect as God is perfect?

Christians lived for the afterlife, not for the trials they faced during this lifetime. During Galileo's time, life was very difficult. Knowing there was a better life awaiting us was the comfort religion offered the masses. Galileo's theories stood to remove this comfort and leave the populace with little regard or trust in all that had been taught, and then chaos would ensue, or so it was thought. With no punishment and reward offered for a life of sin or righteousness, what motivation would one have for remaining moral?

By experience we find we live better, happier, more joyful lives on Earth by following the laws of nature that have been discovered. Are there more laws of nature we are yet to discover? Be ready for new discoveries as God's plan continues to unfold!

> [14]I press on toward the goal to win the prize for which
> God has called me heavenward in Christ Jesus.
>
> –Philippians 3:14 (New International Version)

CHAPTER 13

KARL MARX: CHANGING
THE WORLD WITH THOUGHT

*If you work hard on developing your virtues, you will
not only be successful, you will be happy when you get
there. Success is no protection against depression, but
virtuous actions are. Virtues are like patience, kindness,
forgiveness, tolerance, compassion, and responsibility.
Any actions that you take out of loving-kindness will
register on your virtue mirror. Your honest intention is
what moves the meter.*

–Harry Palmer

The philosopher, social scientist, historian, and revolutionary Karl Marx is without a doubt the most influential socialist thinker to emerge in the nineteenth century. Although he was largely ignored by scholars in his own lifetime, his social, economic, and political ideas gained rapid acceptance in the socialist movement after his death in 1883. Until quite recently, almost half the population of the world lived under regimes that claimed to be Marxist. This very success, however, has meant that the original ideas of Marx have often been modified and his meanings adapted to a great variety of political circumstances. In addition, the fact that Marx delayed publication of many of his writings meant that it has been only recently that scholars had the opportunity to appreciate Marx's intellectual stature.

Karl Heinrich Marx was born into a comfortable middle-class home in Trier on the river Moselle in Germany on May 5, 1818. He came from a long line of rabbis on both sides of his family, and his father, a man who knew Voltaire and Lessing by heart, had agreed to baptism as a Protestant so that he would not lose his job as one of the most respected lawyers in Trier. At the age of 17, Marx enrolled in the Faculty of Law at the University of Bonn. At Bonn, he became engaged to Jenny von Westphalen, the daughter of Baron von Westphalen, a prominent member of Trier society, and man responsible for interesting Marx in Romantic literature and Saint-Simonian politics. The following year, Marx's father sent him to the more serious University of Berlin where he remained for four years, at which time he abandoned his romanticism for the Hegelianism that ruled in Berlin at the time.

Karl Marx, who in the nineteenth century picked up this information, stated that when one force overcomes the other, change is produced. Remember Hegel's dialectical model in the previous chapter? This theory known as *dialectical materialism* stands much like Newton's second law, which states that force is the cause of change in motion and matter is what force acts upon. Marx stated that a revolutionary moment could never be a cooperative venture between the ruling and working classes. For the force of one class must eventually overcome the opposing force of the other class. Two dark clouds spoiled their view. This forced physicists to give up the idea of continuity. Light waves travel without anything to wave in. Hot glowing material emitted a continuous rainbow of light colors that were not explained by the reasonable assumption that light energy was continuously emitted.

Observation of what was happening in the atomic world revealed that observation would disturb the atom, disrupting violently the desire for stasis. It appears that since that quantum leap had discovered that change is inevitable, what we do not see is that we create all change. All change is created when we think thoughts in our minds and release attraction into the world. We change the world. Perhaps we change the world in the direction God would have us change the world, or we change the world in a direction God did not provide but gave us the free will to slightly alter his original plan with the free will he has given us. Need to think about that?

At the turn of the twentieth century, scientist Maxwell Planck pointed out to us that something was wrong with our thinking. It is well past time to keep pace with the obvious advances in science and theology, which are both advancing rapidly. Otherwise, we may find ourselves, as Eric Hoffer said, "beautifully equipped to deal with a world that no longer exists."

> ¹⁵As I began to speak, the Holy Spirit came on them as he had come on us at the beginning. ¹⁶Then I remembered what the Lord had said: "John baptized with[a] water, but you will be baptized with the Holy Spirit." ¹⁷So if God gave them the same gift as he gave us, who believed in the Lord Jesus Christ, who was I to think that I could oppose God? ¹⁸When they heard this, they had no further objections and praised God, saying, "So then, God has granted even the Gentiles repentance unto life."
>
> –Acts 11:15–18 (New International Version)

CHAPTER 14

MAXWELL PLANCK AND NIILS BOHR:
GOD'S SECRETS SEEN
FROM A DIFFERENT VIEW

God rewards those who seek him, not those who seek doctrine or religion or systems or creeds.

–Max Lucado

Maxwell Planck (1858–1947) was born in the midst of what would later be seen as a golden age of Germany. By the time he died, the once great country would be laid to ruins, ravaged by two world wars and the economic depression, political extremism, and international disdain that followed them.

But in the mid-nineteenth century, when Planck came of age, Germany was flourishing. It was a cultural mecca for sophisticated Europeans, a center of literature, philosophy, culture, and, most importantly for Planck, science. The German man was held up as the epitome of the civilized human being. No group benefited more from these heady times than the scientific community, but I add that the nonscientist has much to benefit from learning these ideas, too.

German science led the nineteenth-century charge to discover the fundamental workings of the universe. German physicists were second to none, and scientists from all over the world came to study at Germany's prestigious universities. The country's days of glory continued into the early twentieth century. German science, and the reputation of the country as a whole, received a huge boon when Albert Einstein came on the world scene with his theory of relativity. Soon Einstein was the toast of Europe, and Germany came along for the ride. This success was—thanks in part to Planck—closely followed by another, as German physicists led a revolution in physics, developing the new field of quantum mechanics.

Max Planck discovered at the turn of the century what he called a "lucky guess." Fred Alan Wolf describes this discovery for the lay reader in *Taking the Quantum Leap: The New Physics for the Non-Scientist.* Planck's discovery did not take place in a laboratory: it took place in his mind, and he didn't believe it even after Einstein used the idea to explain away another rough edge five years later. He recounted the event 20 years later in 1921, during his Nobel Prize address: "After a few weeks of the most strenuous work in my life, darkness lifted and an unexpected vista began to appear."

This is a case of a scientist having an intellectual breakthrough due to meditation—hard work or strenuously using the brain to find an answer and then, finally, the mind quiets and the answer comes. It is a personal clearing of the sky. The clouds of doubt are slowly replaced with faith in the truth of your dreaming.

Plank found that matter absorbed heat energy and emitted light discontinuously, meaning in lumps. These lumps were totally *unexpected* and *unpredictable*. His magic formula, $E = hf$, though totally unexpected and not justified by any logical mechanical explanation, succeeded in explaining a heretofore unexplained behavior of light and did more for that first time in the history of science. No one was able to really picture what was going on. The mathematical formula had replaced any visual experience. It worked, but it hardly made any sense. Again, we see here the struggle and ultimate success in advancement by explaining the inexplicable.

The biblical explanation of this is much the same. We know that faith works. We know that prayer works. Paul tells us in Colossians 1:4–6 that

> *We always thank God, the Father of our Lord Jesus Christ,*
> *when we pray for you, because we have heard of your faith*
> *in Christ Jesus and of the love you have for all the saints—*
> *the faith and love that spring from the hope that is stored up*
> *for you in heaven and that you have already heard about in*
> *the word of truth, the gospel that has come to you.*

In fact, Paul insists that faith and hope, both such positive emotions, or energy, come from *hope* or our focus on any positive outcome! Do we know how it works? Does it make any sense? As Abraham Lincoln stated, "Belief in things you can see and that in my word makes sense is not faith."

Planck had opened a new vista with this formula. Albert Einstein picked up the formula and gave new insight to the particles of life. Various people I've met have pointed me in what I consider the right direction. Great thinkers of our time such as Sam Farina, Gerry Robert, Jack Canfield, Bob Proctor, Earl Nightingale, Jim Rohn, Zig Zigler, Bruce Naylor, Ralph Faudree, John Assaraf, Murray Smith, Bill Harris, Bruce Wilkinson, Robert Schuller, Hale Dwoskin, John Maxwell, Franklin Graham, Rick Warren, Stephen Covey, Wayne Dyer, and Mark Victor Hansen have not only entered into my circle of influence, but have shown me great insight and a new way of understanding God's plan in my life, which I would like to share with you, my reader.

So the door that Planck opened early in the twentieth century showed that wave particles are granules of light. How can this be if light is seemingly intangible? We cannot hold a beam of light, so how can there be granules associated with it? It goes back to the idea that everything in the universe, the entire cosmos created by God, is made up of energy that *can* be measured.

All things in physics, the study that leads us to the understanding of energy, matter, space, and time, are divided into *units*, much like the dollar bill, which can be divided into 100 pennies or 10 dimes, 20 nickels or four quarters, or a combination of all of them, and then the dollar itself is a unit. We can expand this in the other direction where a one dollar bill is one tenth of the ten dollar bill, and so on. This is how our universe is set up, too. The universe seems to go on infinitely in its largesse and in its quantum properties as well.

Planck's "universal constant" was also a unit that could be made of other units. Moving objects "join" or connect when they pass a fixed point in space. In other words, they congregate. I think it is a very interesting analogy. Just as like-minded people join in congregations to share their similar beliefs and learn more, other objects, such as atoms, also congregate to form larger units called *matter*. These congregations of particles begin to move and whirl in a circle. Angular momentum can be thought of as momentum moving in a circle. It is much like kids playing with a tetherball hanging from a pole. They jump and swing in a circle around the pole by hanging on to the tether, exhibiting their angular momentum.

Another interesting concept is from Niels Bohr, a Danish physicist of the same period, who theorized that electrons moved in fixed orbits around an atom's nucleus, and he explained how they emitted or absorbed energy. He also posed the idea of "quantum jumps." The best picture Bohr came up with was that a quantum jump, or a leap (and you may remember the 1980s television show called *Quantum Leap* about a scientist who was able to cross time in order to set things right) from one place to another without passing through the space in between, was possible. It seems unreasonable to us because it replaces the classical, mechanical picture of that process.

Does this involve Zeno the philosopher in Ancient Greece who lived from 336 to 224 BC? In Zeno's view, inner peace was reached when a person accepted life as it was, knowing that the world was rationally organized by the *logos*. A person's mind should control his or her emotions and body so that one could live according to the rational principles of the world. This philosophy, called *Stoicism*, became very influential under Roman officials. It seemed to combine Greek philosophy with Jewish mysticism. Universal truths were being uncovered by thinkers of vastly different backgrounds yet who all sought to know God.

Bohr noted that by calculating the change in orbits between large atomic diameter orbits and small diameter orbits, agreement with classically predicted Newtonian principles results. In other words, the smaller the relative changes, the more classical and continuous the results seem to be. Bohr determined another exciting feature of quantum mechanics. It applied just where it was necessary. Wherever the world appeared to be, continuous quantum rules corresponded with classic rules. This is called the *principle of correspondence* in quantum physics. Bohr believed he was on to one of God's secrets. He knew why the world appeared continuous even though it was fundamentally a discontinuous and quantum-leaping world. It was a question of relative scale. To Bohr, discontinuity or chaos was a fundamental truth. However, an order could be found when seeking answers from another viewpoint. We can look at things from a religious perspective and a scientific perspective and get different views, but what is the message there? Is our universe set up to show us what we need to see at a given moment from the approach we take?

It seems Bohr got to a place in his understanding that some things are indeed inexplicable and therefore must have a higher guidance if particles react differently by simply observing them in a different manner. When we take a different perspective, we see something different or in another light. How profound if we apply this to our lives, our surroundings, our families, and even scripture. What is it you wish to see? Can you look at the black sheep of the family with love and see a beautiful human being? Is there some goodness there? I dare say, if we change our observations of everything and everyone around us, we will indeed see something different as Bohr's "complimentary principle" suggests. Look for the good.

Consider the following poem by Emily Dickenson, "When a Particle Is a Wave":

> *I never saw a moor, I never saw the sea, yet I know how*
> *the heather looks and what a wave must be*

We need not be able to see, feel, or touch something to know that it is so. That is what is done through faith. And in science, we see the continuing surrender to "matters of faith."

> [4]because we have heard of your faith in Christ Jesus and of the love you have for all the saints— [5]the faith and love that spring from the hope that is stored up for you in heaven and that you have already heard about in the word of truth, the gospel [6]that has come to you. All over the world this gospel is bearing fruit and growing, just as it has been doing among you since the day you heard it and understood God's grace in all its truth.
>
> –Colossians 1:4–6 (New International Version)

CHAPTER 15

ALBERT EINSTEIN: LAME SCIENCE
AND BLIND RELIGION

> *Imagination is more important than knowledge.*
>
> **–Albert Einstein**

Einstein's theory of relativity is often lost on adults, but children are getting it! This may be one reason why many churches are losing membership. Kids are smarter these days and leave their parents behind when it comes to understanding new concepts. The lack of understanding of how scripture supports this scientific breakthrough is one cause for the declining numbers in religion. If priests and pastors could learn to teach it more effectively, we would see, in my opinion, an increase in participation in churches.

In the words of Albert Einstein, "Science without religion is lame. Religion without science is blind." It is this very concept that resonates so deeply within me that I decided to write a book. Probably one of the greatest minds of all time, Albert Einstein was born at Ulm, in Württemberg, Germany, on March 14, 1879. The family moved to Munich, where he later began his schooling at the Luitpold Gymnasium. They then moved to Italy, and Albert continued his education at Aarau, Switzerland, and in 1896, he entered the Swiss Federal Polytechnic School in Zurich to be trained as a teacher in physics and mathematics. In 1901, the year he gained his diploma, he acquired Swiss citizenship and, as he was unable to find a teaching post—in retrospect, this is amusing—he accepted a position as technical assistant in the Swiss Patent Office. Can you imagine denying Albert Einstein a teaching position? In 1905, he obtained his doctoral degree.

During his stay at the patent office, and in his spare time, he produced much of his remarkable work, and in 1908, he was appointed privatdozent (academic without full professorship) in Berne. In 1909, he became professor extraordinary at Zurich. In 1911, he become professor of theoretical physics at Prague and returned to Zurich in the following year to fill a similar post. In 1914, he was appointed director of the Kaiser Wilhelm Physical Institute and professor at the University of Berlin. He became a German citizen in 1914 and remained in Berlin until 1933, when he renounced his citizenship for political reasons and emigrated to America to take the position of professor of theoretical physics at Princeton. He became a United States citizen in 1940 and retired from his post in 1945.

After World War II, Einstein was a leading figure in the World Government Movement. He was offered the presidency of the State of Israel, which he declined, and he collaborated with Dr. Chaim Weizmann in establishing the Hebrew University of Jerusalem.

Einstein always appeared to have a clear view of the problems of physics and the determination to solve them. He had a strategy of his own and was able to visualize the main stages on the way to his goal. He regarded his major achievements as mere stepping-stones for the next advance.

At the start of his scientific work, Einstein realized the inadequacies of Newtonian mechanics, and his special theory of relativity stemmed from an attempt to reconcile the laws of mechanics with the laws of the electromagnetic field. He dealt with classical problems of statistical mechanics and problems in which they were merged with quantum theory: this led to an explanation of the Brownian movement of molecules. He investigated the thermal properties of light with a low radiation density, and his observations laid the foundation of the photon theory of light. Science, especially quantum physics, has made tremendous progress in our awareness of the cosmos, but Einstein realized and stated emphatically that we cannot and never will explain the divine force behind creation.

Einstein set out to construct a set of unified field theories to explain how the universe worked in the 1920s and spent much of his life in solitude devoted to this endeavor.

In 1905, while he was working in the patent office, Einstein had four papers published in the *Annaln der Physik*, the leading German physics journal. These are the papers that have become known as the *Annus Mirabilis Papers*.

The first of these was on the topic of the particulate nature of light. It proposed the idea that certain results in experimentation, specifically the photoelectric effect, could be understood simply from the perception that light interacts with matter as discrete "packets" of energy, or quanta, an idea that had been proposed by Planck a few years earlier as a "mathematical manipulation," and which seemed to contradict contemporary wave theories of light. Einstein felt this concept was revolutionary.

Einstein's paper on Brownian motion explained that the random movement of very small, or subatomic particles, was direct evidence of molecular action and as a result supported the "atomic theory." But knowing all of his achievements is a study for a course at a university or even a graduate program. What I feel it is important to know is first that Einstein, like many of the great prophets of scripture, was without acknowledgment in his homeland first, and then by the scientific community for a while.

Though most students of science, even middle-school-age children, recognize $E = mc^2$ as Einstein's theory of relativity, few understand the very simplistic yet phenomenal affect of this quantum revelation. This mathematical formula says tiny amounts of mass could be converted into huge amounts of energy. Put simply, you can make a lot from a little. On an energetic level, we can feed the masses with a few loaves and fish. Einstein's theory of relativity explains a miracle, if you will just broaden your mind for a moment, that Jesus performed. It needs to make sense that there is "more than enough" if we have not premeasured the food available when we have the faith in what was taught by Christ. Einstein explained it via scientific observation and mathematics!

In his excellent book, *The Biology of Belief: Unleashing the Power of Consciousness, Matter, and Miracles,* Bruce H. Lipton, PhD, explains to us that "Einstein's theory of relativity shows us that THE UNIVERSE is one indivisible dynamic whole in which energy and matter are so deeply entangled it is impossible to consider them as independent elements." Because Jesus knew this, he had *no problem* feeding the masses. Did Jesus simply split atoms on some level and create more? Jesus attributed his miracles to his Father, so by the manipulation of the universal energy, Jesus used the power of God to perform an action later proved doable by science. As Lipton points out, Einstein showed us that energy and matter are so entwined that we can't really separate them, so if Jesus used God's power to feed the masses, and it's all connected, then is that support for an omnipresent God? And let's not forget, Jesus performed his miracles in the first century for the greater good—to feed the masses. Humans figured out how to destroy using this idea in the twentieth century. Through the power of understanding these principles, however, we can learn to use it for good, as Jesus did. And the applications are boundless. With this greater understanding of using energy, there is obviously much more need for ethics and integrity.

Religious Views

It is a common tendency for many humans, especially Westerners, to reject the ideas of another who does not share similar religious or political beliefs. A politician may say something so inherently good and noble yet be rejected for his or her efforts due to political affiliation. Einstein was a Jew. It is important to note, however, that he did not see himself as devout. Being Jewish is an ethnic identity as well as a religious affiliation, and Einstein was Jewish via ethnicity.

Einstein saw the beauty in religiosity and faith and knew that no attempts to explain everything would ever be accomplished via science alone. There is always a need. So, to use an old colloquialism, "let's not throw the baby out with the bathwater."

Einstein wrote in his book, *The World as I See It:*

> *A knowledge of the existence of something we cannot penetrate, of the manifestations of the profoundest reason and the most radiant beauty, which are only accessible to our reason in their most elementary forms—it is this knowledge and this emotion that constitute the truly religious attitude; in this sense and in this alone, I am a deeply religious man.*

To quote the Savior, "Unless you become as little children, you cannot enter the Kingdom of Heaven" (Matt. 18:3). Children see everything good, whether in nature or in their surroundings, with wonder and admiration. On the other hand, if there is something unethical or "bad" around them, they often recognize it before adults do. They trust and know with instinct and faith what supports life and goodness and what does not. Einstein also said, "The most beautiful and profound emotion we can experience is the sensation of the mystical. It is the power of true science." Like children, as we uncover mysteries and they become "truths" provable by scientific inquiry, they need not become less wonderful. They simply become a greater understanding of God's world and how we operate best in it.

For some the term humanist conjures up a knee-jerk reaction similar to hearing the terms *atheist* and *agnostic*. But Einstein also considered himself a *humanist* and was a "supporter of ethical culture." Again, we can reject ideas from their labels, but what is the intention of "ethical culture"? It is to live according to ethics, to live in a manner that is correct and fair to yourself and your community. In fact, the greatest code of ethics ever established and still in use in our law system is presented to Moses in the book of Exodus. It is that list we often refer to as the Ten Commandments. So if humanists really strive for ethical living, why reject that philosophy? There may be other humanist philosophies that do not complement Christian living, but that is where our reasoning, education, and critical-thinking skills come in. In fact, in a paper in *Nature* published in 1940, Einstein wrote his article "Science and Religion," in which he said:

> *A person who is religiously enlightened appears to me to be one who has, to the best of his ability, [not perfectly] liberated himself from the fetters of his selfish desires and is preoccupied with thoughts, feelings, and aspirations to which he clings because of their super-personal value ... regardless of whether any attempt is made to unite this content with a Divine Being.*

Simply put, the best type of religious person is one who walks the walk and isn't so concerned with being able to quote scripture or judge others by their interpretation of the "correct actions." The deeply religious, the true Christian, is one whose actions are not from egoic attachments to being seen as good or "doing God's will." They know what they do is right, to the best of their ability, and they do it simply for that reason.

¹⁵*As evening approached, the disciples came to him and said, "This is a remote place, and it's already getting late. Send the crowds away, so they can go to the villages and buy themselves some food."*

¹⁶*Jesus replied, "They do not need to go away. You give them something to eat." ¹⁷"We have here only five loaves of bread and two fish," they answered. ¹⁸"Bring them here to me," he said. ¹⁹And he directed the people to sit down on the grass. Taking the five loaves and the two fish and looking up to heaven, he gave thanks and broke the loaves. Then he gave them to the disciples, and the disciples gave them to the people. ²⁰They all ate and were satisfied, and the disciples picked up twelve basketfuls of broken pieces that were left over. ²¹The number of those who ate was about five thousand men, besides women and children.*

–Matthew 14:15–21 (New International Version)

CHAPTER 16

THE PRACTICE OF MEDITATION

The best things in life are free.

–Anonymous

Meditation has been used by some of the greatest scientific and religious minds over the centuries, leading to stunning breakthroughs in ideas and thought. The practice of meditation is simply the clearing of the mind of all thoughts so that you can focus on one idea or issue at a time. This is one reason that many great scientists and religious icons such as Jesus were often noted to spend hours in solitude, giving their whole being to focused thought or prayer concerning one issue. Jesus spent many days, weeks, and months of solitude with fasting and prayer to clarify the truths he eventually came to teach. These were often radical for his day and required great courage.

The same is true of scientists. I've made quite clear the fact that many of the founding fathers of the scientific revolution around the world were reluctant participants. Given that they could have been ostracized or even killed for heresy due to their radical ideas, they tended to toil away in the shadows and in solitude—which ironically allowed them to concentrate and focus on the new theories uninterrupted.

Meditation can be used by anyone for any reason, even to overcome a problem area in one's life. Though my medical practice has brought me joy and fulfillment, I've always added travel to my life. For many years, I've volunteered in the Dominican Republic as well as at my church and in other charitable organizations. But I do not want to discount the contribution my travels have made in my life, especially travel to those lands where spirituality takes a form radically different from our Western Christianity and philosophies.

From the time of my first visit to Egypt, I had always wanted to go inside a large pyramid at Giza and learn more about it and why it was built. By many people, it was felt to be a burial place for a pharaoh. There is some controversy about whether it was indeed a burial place or if it was a place for initiates in a spiritual journey.

I recently had an opportunity to return to Egypt on more of a spiritual-type journey. I had the pleasure of going through the pyramid. Before returning to Egypt, I had a dream. In my dream, I was in fear of being trapped within a pyramid and unable to get out. I had this dream or this feeling intermittently over a six-month period prior to going. It became very strong the morning that we were leaving to go into the pyramid. I elected to feel the fear and go anyway, which is also the title of a book I have read. I began to think as I was getting dressed that I should face this fear and share it with my roommate in our travels along with 60 people, and an Egyptian spiritual expert. I told him about my dream about being trapped within a pyramid. He listened, and we discussed it briefly. A miracle occurred. The fear left when I began to be open and talk about it, ready to move forward into the structure.

As we approached the pyramid, I had *no more fear,* and we discussed what was within it. There are three rooms and a 4 foot by 4 foot passageway down into the lower room. Traversing it required a little bit of stooping, but it was wide enough so that you could pass another person without a problem. It took about ten minutes to get in and go down to the lower room below the level of the base of the pyramid. The room was large enough that the 50 people or so in attendance could easily find a place to sit propped up against the rocks in the full area of the room. There was a large hole, probably 10 to 12 feet across, and it was 10 feet deep in one area, and then went on down into what appeared to be a black hole.

In one corner of the room, there was a small passageway that would be more difficult to maneuver through, which went right under the peak of the pyramid. You could look up and view the top. Seven people were selected to go in and a meditation was begun.

This lower part of the lower room was considered to be the place to release from the unconscious mind to recognize the dark side for each person in this area. There was a quietness as we sat there, and the purpose in this room was for the initiate to release and leave behind the beliefs that no longer served the initiate and to carry those things that the unconscious mind directed to the edge of the deep pit and to release them into the pit and no longer be a part of what was holding you back from where God would have you be. There was some crying as this occurred.

It is interesting to note that in meditation it is very important to remember and to learn that it's what you bring to meditation that creates a successful period of meditation. If you bring quiet and science, being still, and knowing that God is with you, you will have a very successful meditation. The Psalm 46:10, "Be still and know that I am God," suggests that it is essential to release God and to listen to what he is telling you, which may come quickly or slowly. It may require two or three returns to a meditation to receive the release and finding of the paradigms that are not serving you well in achieving God's purpose for your life. Though this experience is not a specifically Christian one, I felt it as profound as any I've had in Christian-based spiritual exercises, for ultimately it was a personal experience of God in the way I see him, relate to him, and choose to receive his communications.

After our meditation experience, we climbed back up to where we could move into the second room, which was not a large room. It was big enough so that our crowd of 60 people could have gotten into it, but it was more difficult to sit in this room for meditation. This room was felt to be related to our conscious mind as opposed to our unconscious mind, which was thought to be the purpose for the lower chamber. In this room, we began to deal with our expectations, goals, and things that we wanted to achieve as they formed in our minds. We walked around clockwise when we entered the room, thinking about our ambitions, and then left the room and moved up to the top room, which was larger—I would estimate the room approximately 20 feet by 30 feet with a sarcophagus at one end. We began an "eyes closed meditation," including chanting while we were there for about an hour and a half.

The temperature in the upper room was warmer than in the two lower ones but not unbearably hot. During the chanting, we noted the vibration and the change of vibration with different types of chants. We had a period of meditation and then each of us had an opportunity to "die to our old self" by getting into the sarcophagus for 30 seconds to contemplate beginning a new life. This ritual reminds us that we must die to the old to grow and begin anew. It is a great way to recognize yourself and your current needs, which may have outgrown your needs of a different time in your life. This was, overall, a phenomenal experience in a place built in 2500 BC (4500) that is still intact and used on occasion, perhaps, as it was intended.

Another experience I had occurred while visiting China. We had a large celebration at a Buddhist temple near the hotel where we were staying. We went to this celebration, and there was a large fire burning in the central courtyard. Paper was being burned as the people sought forgiveness and forward movement in their lives. Some were crying, and some were happy. I noticed one lady who looked very dower and was crying large tears; obviously she was very uncomfortable. She brought her problems and left them in the fire. Essentially, she gave them to God.

In Jerusalem, it was interesting to see the "wailing wall," which is a remnant of the base of the Temple of Solomon. People bring their problems to the wall written on a small piece of paper and place it in a crevice. These could be positive requests, goals, or a prayer for others—anything you want to write to leave in the hands of God. You bring your happiness or fear or thoughts to God and turn them loose by putting the message in the wall. There were many people there. Again, some were happy, some crying, and some fearful, but if they brought their problem or goal to the wall and left it, with faith it will be resolved.

In meditation, regardless of type, the importance is what you bring to the meditation to fully release (holding on to it suggests you don't think God can handle it!) by throwing it in the pit, as in the room deep within the pyramid, or by burning it at the Buddhist temple, or a list of things in your heart and life that are more related to your dark side, or leaving the paper in the wall of the temple. All are simply different ways of ridding yourself of worry—things from within that were left there by mother, father, relative, fear, or worry—all ways of leaving behind and moving forward in achieving God's purpose for your life. I've even heard of people having their own worry jars where they write down their fears and label the jar "God." It is a physical action to help our brains learn to let go of the worry, which can lead to stress and disease. But essentially and eventually, it must be turned over if correct communication is to be returned to you to resolve your dilemma.

³⁶*Then Jesus went with his disciples to a place called Gethsemane, and he said to them, "Sit here while I go over there and pray."* ³⁷*He took Peter and the two sons of Zebedee along with him, and he began to be sorrowful and troubled.* ³⁸*Then he said to them, "My soul is overwhelmed with sorrow to the point of death. Stay here and keep watch with me."* ³⁹*Going a little farther, he fell with his face to the ground and prayed, "My Father, if it is possible, may this cup be taken from me. Yet not as I will, but as you will."*

–Matthew 26:36–39 (New International Version)

CHAPTER 17

THOUGHTS CREATE THE UNIVERSE

What lies behind us and what lies before us are tiny matters compared to what lies within us.

–Ralph Waldo Emerson

The seven laws of quantum physics are a group of "laws" about which I am very inspired. They make sense to me both as a scientist and physician and as a theologian on a spiritual path. The first of these laws, the Law of Perpetual Transmutation of Energy, shows how **energy moves into physical form**. Therefore, if everything is indeed energy, then the images you hold in your mind most often materialize in your results in your life— both good and bad. But this is not a new concept at all, even for the most devout Christians. We can find this theme using scripture from both the Old and New Testaments of the Holy Bible. In the beginning, in Genesis, it is *God's thinking and speaking* that brings creation into existence—"and He saw that it was good."

Super laws are like gravity: they work in every centimeter of the universe all the time. The seven super laws are applications and expressions of quantum physics. Quantum physics is a branch of science and gives us the understanding of the seven laws that apply to everyone. That is, these laws apply regardless of your status in the world, good or bad, regardless of level of intelligence, regardless of vocabulary, faith, belief, thoughts, emotion, and action, through understanding of the laws of quantum physics. This is also regardless of language, regardless of climate, and regardless of teaching. The laws of quantum physics are like gravity; it is the way God created the earth. Gravity is a rule we all know; it applies to every one of us. This law can be challenged by jumping from any height, and you will fall. Gravity always works the same way for everything and everyone.

Recent major earthquakes in the mountains of China caused buildings to collapse, bridges to fall down, and rocks to roll or fall down the mountainside, crushing the roads. People, schools, buildings, and rocks fell regardless of size or weight. Everything shaken loose by the earthquake fell, crushing whatever was below. Nothing escaped, regardless of status. The destruction of the quake loosened the earthly materials, and they were pulled down, showing no favoritism.

So I stand behind the one great law of quantum physics, and that is: Everything is energy. Energy is motion. Energy never stands still. It takes one form, then another. Change is all there is.

An article by Mitch Harvictz references Neville Goddard, "An Influential Thought Teacher," who had several sayings that are keys to understanding these new concepts. These are not new occurrences, but new ways of looking at what has occurred throughout the history of the world. "[Because of] the power of awareness, the Lord of hosts will not respond to your wish until you have assumed the feeling of already being what you want to be for *expectance* is the channel of His action."

The universe is made of pure energy, the nature of which is to move and flow. The nature of life is constant change, constant flux. When we understand this, we tune into its rhythm, and we are able to give and receive freely, knowing that we never really lose anything, but constantly gain or transform from one state of existence to another.

There is a "thinking stuff from which all things are made," and which, in its original state, permeates, penetrates, and fills the interspaces of the universe. A thought in this substance produces the thing that is imagined by the thought. In other words, what we think is what occurs or "shows up" in our lives. If we think good, life-affirming thoughts about ourselves and others, that is what appears. If we think negative, destructive thoughts about ourselves and our situations and circumstances, we get more of that, too. It's like sending out little prayers that get answered; yet you may not have even realized that any being, especially *God,* was paying attention to what you were thinking. Words and actions affect this process at an exponential rate. If we speak negatively or positively, that creates the situations even faster or in a manner that may simply validate the words. Children, for example, live up to the expectations we set for them. It is no coincidence that children who are encouraged are often successful adults. But there is a time when we can no longer use the excuses of our childhood in our adult world, especially once we've been made aware of the reality that exists with this law of the transmutation of energy. We are responsible for our own lives. We begin to change our circumstances when we accept that our choices, our free will, have been the major factor in creating the lives we live today.

Neville Goddard also said:

> *Leave the mirror and change your face. Leave the world*
> *alone and change your conception of yourself. Your faith*
> *is your fortune. Do not try to change people; they are*

only messengers telling you who you are. Revalue yourself
and they will confirm the change. Your faith is
your fortune.

Neville Goddard's Experience with Negative Thought.

Neville wanted to go to Barbados for Christmas from New York to be with his large family who still lived there. His friend who lived in New York was an Ethiopian scholar who was filled with spirituality. He told Neville, "Live as though you are there, and that you shall be." He waited a bit, but he remained faithful to the assumption that he was in Barbados and had traveled first class.

On a December morning before the last ship was to depart from New York that year for Barbados, Neville received a letter from a long out-of-touch brother. With it was fifty dollars and a ticket to sail. The experiment, it seemed, had worked. It is not what you want that you attract, but you attract what you believe to be true and having faith knowing it will happen. Neville offered his listeners and readers meditative techniques such as using the power of visualization before going to sleep. He noted that, "I do believe that one must completely saturate himself with visualization of things expected from God through Faith and belief in the word of God before his visualization is manifested for you. "This resonates through many spiritual traditions of the world. One cannot renounce what one has not obtained to move beyond the material world such as its wealth; one must know wealth.

Psalms 82:6 states, "Ye are God—the literal truth of man's condition." Likewise, Proverbs 16:9 tells us, "The mind of man plans his way, but the Lord directs his steps." God speaks to us through the Bible, through mediation, and through prayer for guidance. We can see this by those who truly practice it and live it in their lives. One of the great contemporary Christian theologians tells us, using a beautiful analogy, how to obtain the peace in our lives so many of us desire. Robert Schuller speaks on surrender when he asks:

How do you catch a dove? If you want to catch a dove, you reach out your hand cautiously, slowly, and leave your hand extended, holding it straight in front of you with an open palm. Be quiet, and the dove will come and rest right in the middle of your hand. If you want God's direction, surrender your soul, your mind, and your spirit in the same way a dove surrenders to an open hand. If you do, God will take over your life and guide you.

[6]"I said, "'You are 'gods'; you are all sons of
the Most High."

–Psalm 82:6 (New International Version)

[9] In his heart a man plans his course, but the LORD
determines his steps.

–Proverbs 16:9 (New International Version)

CHAPTER 18

RELATIVELY SPEAKING: IT'S NEITHER REALLY GOOD NOR BAD

> *The only thing we have to fear is fear itself.*
>
> **–Franklin D. Roosevelt**

Everything in our material world is made real by its relationship to something else. We can understand hot because we can compare it to cold. In science, we group things in species, genuses, classes, and so on based on how close or different they are to other natural occurrences. Some animals, though half a world away, share similar traits to others and are considered relatives on a very basic level. So too are ethnic groups, cultures, religions, and many other groupings of people and things. Relationships are everything, and everything is due to its relationship with other things. The Law of Relativity states that **nothing is good or bad, big or small, et cetera, until you relate it to something else.**

For example, if a woman is five foot four and her friends are five foot three, is she short among her friends or tall? But if you compare her to a woman who is six feet tall, she is apparently short! If you practice relating your situation to something much worse, yours will always look good, but beware of focusing too much on the bad. There is no need to be or feel guilty because you are blessed. Practicing gratitude is a great way to learn to work with the law of relativity.

In addition to gratitude, adopting an attitude of nonjudgment is tremendously helpful in spiritual growth. Though we are to embrace and care for our fellow humans, it is not our job to police them, whether it is lifestyle, income, or educational levels or any other issue specific to learning to love and accept other humans, including other collective groups such as religious denominations, nations, races, and even those difficult neighbors and relatives.

Relativity is a democratizer. It does tell us of bizarre esoteric qualities, but in a nutshell, we are all equal. Take, for example, mythical stories from various cultures. Many people, for example, in Asia and Europe, believed in dragons, though we now know them to be fantasy creatures.

Like dragons, many cultures believed in giants, though giants we can now see may be a "freak of nature" that occurs with physiological explanations. We're all familiar with the story of David and Goliath, a giant whose name is now synonymous with "giant." So whether the concepts are mythical in nature as was St. George and the Dragon or scientifically possible such as a small boy learning to work with a weapon to take down a human larger than his people had ever seen, there are similar stories, beliefs, and values inherent cross-culturally.

Most religions share similarities on some level. If we look for similarities in our fellow humans, we will find them, for we usually find that which we seek. Looking for how we are connected versus how we are separated by differences is a wonderful way to practice Christian charity and begin to feel that "agape" love described so beautifully by the apostle John. The notion of love for all humans on a pure level is what will make us feel connected and as one unified family, congregation, nation, or world. All states in the universe are an equal notion. We are not superior to those who do not share our beliefs. We simply know a different way to be. We must be the change we want to see in the world and lead by example.

In his book, *Biology of Belief: Unleashing the Power of Consciousness, Matter, and Miracles,* Bruce Lipton explains Einstein's theory of relativity succinctly. He states:

Energy (E) = Matter (m, mass) multiplied by the Speed of Light squared (c^2). Einstein revealed that we do not live in a universe with discrete, physical objects separated by dead space. The Universe is *one indivisible, dynamic whole* in which energy and matter are so deeply entangled it is impossible to consider them as independent elements.

$E = mc^2$—we're all equal, and we all see physics the same no matter where we live on the planet or who we choose to worship.

Instructions on Worship

[1]*I urge, then, first of all, that requests, prayers, intercession and thanksgiving be made for everyone— [2]for kings and all those in authority, that we may live peaceful and quiet lives in all godliness and holiness. [3]This is good, and pleases God our Savior, [4]who wants all men to be saved and to come to a knowledge of the truth. [5]For there is one God and one mediator between God and men, the man Christ Jesus, [6]who gave himself as a ransom for all men—the testimony given in its proper time. [7]And for this purpose I was appointed a herald and an apostle—I am telling the truth, I am not lying—and a teacher of the true faith to the Gentiles.*

–1 Timothy 2:1–7 (New International Version)

CHAPTER 19

DOWN ON YOUR LUCK? SUPER!
JUST CHANGE DIRECTIONS

> *There are two ways to live your life. One is as though nothing is a miracle. The other is as if everything is.*
>
> **–Albert Einstein**

Nothing can exist without its opposite. It is so clearly demonstrated in the ancient text, Ecclesiastes. If hate exists in someone, then love must exist as well. It is clearly evident, to nearly everyone, that we are currently in a period of economic hardship, again, and we've been at war far longer than we expected, just like Vietnam. As has occurred throughout history, we find ourselves in an apparent state of moral and ethical decline in society shown vividly by our politicians whose lives are fraught with scandal displayed before us in the media. The parallels from bygone eras are uncanny. We cannot know one of these concepts, good and bad, prosperity and poverty, and so on, or understand one without the other, though as adults we can remember the painful experiences of youth and choose to feel differently toward one another and use our life experience to create a brighter future. That's wisdom. We can guide children and young people to hopefully learn from our experiences, but ultimately we know everyone must learn lessons on his or her own.

When I was a sophomore in college, I recognized the closeness between love and hate as emotions. It is a painful awareness to recognize, but this is indeed an example of the Law of Polarity—it is difficult to know success without failure or perceived failure.

The Law of Polarity tells us that **every thing has *an opposite:* male-female, (yin/yang) hot-cold, health-sickness, good-bad, inside-outside, short-tall, wealth-poverty, and so on.** These polarized concepts are part of our natural world and are often similar to the idea of relativity. Do you ever wonder why in a world of unfathomable abundance, we must sometimes go through events, conditions, and circumstances that we perceive as unpleasant such as war, a volatile economy, or redefined morals and ethics? Some have even proposed the idea of rewriting the United States Constitution. This very suggestion has caused a fight among Americans who have very solid opinions on the matter, but without these polarized ideas, how could we even examine our laws and options in the matter? The opposing opinions are what will allow us as a society to arrive at something better.

Many great teachers of our time are working diligently to help others remain hopeful in what seems to be an era of despair. In an email sent out on December 18, 2008, James Ray shares some profound insights into the state of the world and how we will not only survive it but how to see this time as necessary. Ray writes about esoteric principles and ideas:

> *Contrary to popular opinion, all things esoteric are not voodoo or mumbo-jumbo. Interestingly enough, math and science were once esoteric teachings and only taught to the king, his family and his inner court.* **All is in harmony, and perfectly orchestrated.** *We've just moved into winter in our world, which is fitting as the winter of 2008 approaches. By the way, for those naysayers and doomsday prophets—this is not the first "winter" of our economic life. The US has had six economic winters since the 1950s.*

I think it is vital to remember what he is saying to keep things in perspective. For many, it is the first economic hardship on such a scale, and for others, we've weathered several. Each time we fear it is "the big one." But as we grow personally and spread our newfound knowledge, apply just a few principles that support our personal growth and help others to do the same. We'll find that we're more resilient than we were in the 1970s or 1980s or even earlier. Things are moving much more quickly. If the decline was rapid, the recovery can occur quickly, too. The economy can make a quantum leap. Remember the dot-com boom then bust of the late1980s and 1990s? The concept of the Internet caught on so quickly that many people became wealthy overnight. Just as quickly, many lost what they'd gained, but after this occurrence, things evened out to where the Internet is as common in every home as the television was in the 1980s.

This idea of a situation developing and then swinging to its polar opposite to usher in positive cultural and philosophical evolution was defined for us by the nineteenth-century German philosopher G. W. F. Hegel in his teachings on dialectics. Hegel starts with a "thesis" or situation the way it is now. In our example, it is the sudden business boom of the Internet age. With the dot-com bust, we see an "antithesis," which is radical and painful. People lost millions and went belly up. But the Internet did not collapse nor did our entire economic structure. In fact, today we have a more stabilized investment strategy when dealing with Internet business. This new, improved way of operating is what Hegel called "synthesis." And the exciting yet often frightening thing about this way of describing the progress of society is that once we arrive at a synthesis, we begin the process all over with a thesis. And we move forward. James Ray's recent communication encourages us that this is so. He emphasizes:

> *Winter is never a time to despair. Quite the contrary,*
> *coming from a long run of sowing and reaping, it's now*
> *time to regroup, to reflect upon the lessons learned, to*
> *possibly spend more time with our family in celebration*
> *of what we've accomplished and most definitely plan*
> *for our next spring.*

James Ray goes on to say that we may wish for sunnier times, but essentially, the seasons come and go because that is nature's way. Being negative in "winter," whether it is the naturally occurring season or just a hard time in our lives financially, economically or even emotionally, will do us no good. We will "survive" the winter better if we understand this is the plan and keep our thoughts and actions positive and upbeat. Smile. Smiles can change your day and the day of those around you. It's been said that you're more likely to get good customer service in retail establishments if you start the exchange with a smile.

There are numerous actions you can take to lessen the effects of a downturn in your internal emotions or external circumstances. One of my favorites is to remember and relive those happy times. Even in the face of an unexpected death or tragic loss, remembering the good and happy times can help you feel better and have a more positive outlook.

We each have those places that help us feel alive and inspired. It doesn't have to be a pyramid in Gaza, but it can be! For some, it is a mountain stream communing with trout, for others, a cup of coffee on their back porch watching the sun come up. Whether it is a walk through a park or watching the fish in a pond, take the time to fill your inspirational well. Allow yourself to admire the beauty in this world, and in this way, those issues that seem so pressing or overwhelming are made less so.

Live in gratitude. It may seem hard at times to be grateful for all the circumstances you encounter, but each is a step on your own personal journey to a better life, even if it doesn't feel like it sometimes. I have experienced numerous events that might be considered negative, only to find they lead to something good and infinitely more enjoyable than the life I'd previously led. Don't allow yourself to fear change, but embrace it and look forward to what God has in store for you.

A Time for Everything

[1] *There is a time for everything, and a season for every activity under heaven:*

[2] *a time to be born and a time to die, a time to plant and a time to uproot,*

[3] *a time to kill and a time to heal, a time to tear down and a time to build,*

[4] *a time to weep and a time to laugh, a time to mourn and a time to dance,*

[5] *a time to scatter stones and a time to gather them, a time to embrace and a time to refrain,*

[6] *a time to search and a time to give up, a time to keep and a time to throw away,*

[7] *a time to tear and a time to mend, a time to be silent and a time to speak,*

[8] *a time to love and a time to hate, a time for war and a time for peace.*

–Ecclesiastes 3:1–8 (New International Version)

CHAPTER 20

ABRAHAM AND THE LAW OF ATTRACTION

When the going gets tough, the tough get going.

–Joseph P. Kennedy

In the story of Abraham, we see countless examples of God's promises to respond to like treatment with like treatment. This is clearly an example of the Sublaw of Attraction, which states that like attracts like. What we think about, we bring about. This is the case when we direct our thoughts toward others and think either positive things or negative things. For example, in Genesis 12:1–3 we are told:

1 *The LORD had said to Abram, "Leave your country,*
your people and your father's household and go to the
land I will show you.

2 *"I will make you into a great nation*
and I will bless you;
I will make your name great,
and you will be a blessing.

3 *I will bless those who bless you,*
and whoever curses you I will curse;
and all peoples on earth
will be blessed through you."

But Abram had to try it out for himself. I think it is important to note that Abram was a radical figure for his time. It would have been totally unacceptable to first leave the family home and business to follow religious and spiritual ideals, especially those of showing a devotion to *one* god. The people of Abram's time, as we know, were polytheistic and truly believed that the divine beings were much like humans—violent, vindictive, and unforgiving. To show favoritism to one might temporarily bring protection until the status quo shifted and another one may be needed. For example, in a time of war, people would call out to one god, but in a time of famine, another was the better one for the job! But something or someone told Abraham to follow these instructions in order to create the life of his dreams! The story tells us:

4 *So Abram left, as the LORD had told him; and Lot*
went with him. Abram was seventy-five years old when

he set out from Haran. 5 He took his wife Sarai, his nephew Lot, all the possessions they had accumulated and the people they had acquired in Haran, and they set out for the land of Canaan, and they arrived there.

6 Abram traveled through the land as far as the site of the great tree of Moreh at Shechem. At that time the Canaanites were in the land. 7 The LORD appeared to Abram and said, "To your offspring I will give this land." So he built an altar there to the LORD, who had appeared to him.

The building of altars everywhere he set up camp is an interesting analogy. With altars in Abram's time, one showed honor via animal sacrifice, and often human sacrifice, to the divine. So Abram was indeed doing what was ethical for religious practices of his time, and he knew that in order to receive blessings and abundance, he must first give. Tithing is a principle that is similar, for when we tithe, we give in honor of the Lord. Since we know the story of Abram and his evolution to Abraham, we know that the Lord will use him later to radically change the ethics of his time. But God did not sit Abram down in the beginning and say, "OK son! Here is what you have to do. Stop doing *everything* the way you are now and here's a list of how to behave." God gave him instructions slowly and allowed him to test them to see that they work. He allowed Abram to have free will to choose his actions and learn on his own, like a parent does for a child. We would like to spare our children the pain of mistakes, but we know it is often in their best interest to learn on their own.

Abram continues in his journey and eventually lands in Egypt because of famine. By this time he has quite a large entourage and very likely was a force to be reckoned with in terms of population and control of a group. Even in ancient times, large populations moving into an area will upset the politics. Rulers fear overthrow when infiltrated by immigrants. Mass immigration not only greatly affects the economy but political control, too.

This same phenomenon occurred in United States history when the Church of Jesus Christ of Latter Day Saints had a huge settlement in Southern Illinois. Scholars believe that the most logical reason for the execution of the founder of this church in 1846, commonly referred to as the Mormons, was because the number of "saints" or "Mormons" in Nauvoo, Illinois, was large enough to influence the vote, and Joseph Smith could have won the gubernatorial seat for that state. Though their radical practices such as polygamy and rejection of alcohol may have been confronting and immoral for the citizens of the area, the real reason for the hatred and fear of the Mormons was probably much simpler in origin. The people of the areas through which the Mormons traveled and settled, such as Ohio, Missouri, and Illinois, were probably more afraid of the power that could be usurped from those holding office by a large number of citizens who followed a different path. How similar to politics today, don't you think?

Abram experienced good times and bad, and we know that he continued into Egypt because of a severe famine mentioned in Genesis 12:10. The Law of Rhythm tells us that there is and ebb and flow in life. "The tide comes in, and the tide goes out." So this law is related to us in this portion of the story, and it allows Abram the chance to make some choices—to exercise his free will. This may be one of the most confusing stories for some who take it on its surface telling, but when we look deeper, God did not interfere with the decisions of his servant. Actually, he comes in to save him from his own poor choices.

> 11 *As he was about to enter Egypt, he said to his wife*
> *Sarai, "I know what a beautiful woman you are. 12*
> *When the Egyptians see you, they will say, 'This is his*
> *wife.' Then they will kill me but will let you live. 13 Say*
> *you are my sister, so that I will be treated well for your*
> *sake and my life will be spared because of you."*
>
> 14 *When Abram came to Egypt, the Egyptians saw that*
> *she was a very beautiful woman. 15 And when Pharaoh's*
> *officials saw her, they praised her to Pharaoh, and she*

was taken into his palace. 16 He treated Abram well for
her sake, and Abram acquired sheep and cattle, male and
female donkeys, menservants and maidservants,
and camels.

It appears here that Abram was rewarded or paid for the donation of his wife to the Pharoah's harem. But it was not an odd practice for the time and would have actually been a business move or the aligning of politically and economically powerful families. But as we see, when we aren't living in accordance with God's ways, he may redirect our lives. Certainly, the members of Abram's tribes were also affected by plague. We cannot watch those around us suffer and escape the impressions. We don't hear of a major part of the community being affected, but perhaps it is because they may have been living apart from the rest of the community. In any case, Abram is asked to leave the area. Why is this? Maybe this seclusion did save them from contamination, and the lack of understanding of contagious disease made the Egyptians suspicious of the group. Perhaps the only reasonable explanation for this, in Pharoah's mind, was indeed that Abram had the favor of a more powerful god. In any case, Abram leaves Egypt, having increased his overall wealth, which would include gold or other precious metals and stone, healing herbs, animals, and people. He increased the population of his tribe via gifts of humans as slaves and concubines, and his overall wealth increased to a point where the land of Canaan could no longer support such a huge group of nomads. So he split the people and possessions with Lot, and they both went in separate ways.

Lot, too, was a follower of this new way, and though we know his story ends tragically in cities that are now synonymous with immorality, Sodom and Gomorrah, Lot remained true to this new way of life. He followed one God, one universal guidance.

A major issue of importance with Abram, however, is shown with the story of Isaac. Child sacrifice was a common practice in Canaan and the entire ancient world. Some areas continued to practice this publicly well into the Middle Ages as a way to appease the gods. It was expected. Abraham, as he is called later, is told by God to stop the practice. He is saved from committing this act. In other words, we once again see this man asked to do something that is radically different from the accepted practices of the day.

We can look to Abraham's example any time we are faced with an issue that is considered "OK because it is what everyone is doing," and yet we know in our hearts that it is wrong. God will reveal the correct course of action if we just listen. And to listen to the words of God, we must have moments of silence and meditation, for when our minds are too busy, he cannot get through to us. We, by continuously cluttering our minds with a barrage of thoughts, whatever they may be, are exercising our free will. Clear your mind and let him speak.

We can find similar examples of the universal laws in other biblical stories. Moses is another figure whose radical departure from the norms of society shows that in order to initiate change, we must take action. With Moses, too, we get a new way of operating, or ethics, when he is allowed to visit with God and receive specific instructions on what is right and wrong. He begins to contemplate the results of his actions early in his adult life. In Exodus we are told:

> 11 *One day, after Moses had grown up, he went out to where his own people were and watched them at their hard labor. He saw an Egyptian beating a Hebrew, one of his own people.* 12 *Glancing this way and that and seeing no one, he killed the Egyptian and hid him in the sand.* 13 *The next day he went out and saw two Hebrews fighting. He asked the one in the wrong, "Why are you hitting your fellow Hebrew?"*
>
> 14 *The man said, "Who made you ruler and judge over us? Are you thinking of killing me as you killed the Egyptian?" Then Moses was afraid and thought, "What I did must have become known."*

Our actions are constantly judged by others. Moses knew this and was indeed a public figure, yet he aligned himself with the Hebrew slaves and made himself subject to their criticism. His fleeing of Egypt from the wrath of Pharaoh was a self-preservation action, but the Lord needed him in a state of reflection in order to communicate his instructions for a new way of being, that which is given to us through the Ten Commandments. Moses's fleeing to the desert and escape from society was his way of meditating in order to hear the call of God. And because most of us are very familiar with the aspects of this story, we know that the instructions given to Moses required action on his part and also determination.

Pharaoh did not let go of the slaves easily. To do so would upset the economy and halt progress on the projects he had them working on, in addition to their being the very foundation of the economic system. But eventually, God gave him instructions to save the people from a plague of the worst kind. How Moses knew the healing and protection property of hyssop in the protection against disease is probably the basis for the miracle, but evidently he knew something the Egyptians did not. He was immunizing the Hebrews against the infection, and we read about this in the following passage.

> 21 Then Moses summoned all the elders of Israel and
> said to them, "Go at once and select the animals for
> your families and slaughter the Passover lamb. 22 Take
> a bunch of hyssop, dip it into the blood in the basin and
> put some of the blood on the top and on both sides of the
> doorframe. Not one of you shall go out the door of his
> house until morning. 23 When the LORD goes through
> the land to strike down the Egyptians, he will see the
> blood on the top and sides of the doorframe and will pass
> over that doorway, and he will not permit the destroyer
> to enter your houses and strike you down."

And though this may seem like a neat little tidbit of biblical botany, we see others in the Bible and throughout history use this herb for protection and as a healing herb. I mention this here to show that God has continually chosen to reveal new things to humans in order to make life better, yet humans have chosen to reject some of the simple instructions and instead have chosen to exercise free will, and as is the case of the simple laws of the universe, we see humans have often rejected God's suggestions and instead have chosen to work their will so that where, for example, we may have used the Law of Perpetual Transmutation of Energy to produce things in abundance, instead we created the atom bomb and other nuclear weapons with which we can destroy. Following the simple path and using the instructions given, combined with science applications, has unlimited potential for good, if we will only choose to focus our attention in that direction.

David and the Law of Cause and Effect

The story of King David is one of my favorite stories about the concept of cause and effect, or *karma*. He certainly reaps what he sows. One doesn't have to be perfect, as we've seen with both Abraham, who seemed to cower at the idea of coming up against Pharaoh with a beautiful wife, and Moses, who committed murder and fled in fear, to be called to do the work of God. But despite their special status, they do not escape the laws of quantum physics.

Small children listen to the story of David defeating Goliath with eagerness. A small boy defeats a "giant" using only a rock. Clearly this is another example showing us that Einstein's theory of relativity is true. We can use small amounts of energy to accomplish a gargantuan task if we know how to apply and work with the laws of nature shown to us through biblical analogies. Through his successes, David finds himself anointed as king, as is reported in 2 Samuel 2, but this special status does not exempt him from the Law of Cause and Effect. This law simply states that actions and choices produce a result. For David, in his early life, his choice to trust and his understanding of the laws put him in a place of power. And as we've seen throughout history, sometimes power can corrupt. But though we all know the downfall of David because of his choices to go against the laws of Yahweh as given to Moses, mostly due to committing adultery, David was subject to the consequences of his action, yet he was still a very valuable figure in the Bible. One need not be perfect to do the work of God. In fact, we're all in the same state. When we choose to listen to the call, we can be as effective in our purpose as we choose.

The Call of Abram

[1] *The LORD had said to Abram, "Leave your country, your people and your father's household and go to the land I will show you.* [2]*"I will make you into a great nation and I will bless you; I will make your name great, and you will be a blessing.* [3] *I will bless those who bless you, and whoever curses you I will curse; and all peoples on Earth will be blessed through you."* [4] *So Abram left, as the LORD had told him; and Lot went with him. Abram was seventy-five years old when he set out from Haran.* [5] *He took his wife Sarai, his nephew Lot, all the possessions they had accumulated and the people they had acquired in Haran, and they set out for the land of Canaan, and they arrived there.* [6] *Abram traveled through the land as far as the site of the great tree of Moreh at Shechem. At that time the Canaanites were in the land.*

–Genesis 12:1–6 (New International Version)

CHAPTER 21

JESUS: THE METHOD AND THE MAN

The best and most beautiful things in the world cannot be seen or even touched. They must be felt with the heart.

–Anonymous

286. O Sacred Head Now Wounded

Text: *Anonymous; trans. by Paul Gerhardt and James W. Alexander*
Music: *Hans L. Hassler, 1564–1612; harm. by J.S. Bach, 1685–1750*
Tune: *PASSION CHORALE,* **Meter:** *76.76 D*

1. O sacred Head, now wounded,
with grief and shame weighed down,
now scornfully surrounded
with thorns, thine only crown:
how pale thou art with anguish,
with sore abuse and scorn!
How does that visage languish
which once was bright as morn!

2. What thou, my Lord, has suffered
was all for sinners' gain;
mine, mine was the transgression,
but thine the deadly pain.
Lo, here I fall, my Savior!
'Tis I deserve thy place;
look on me with thy favor,
vouchsafe to me thy grace.

3. What language shall I borrow
to thank thee, dearest friend,
for this thy dying sorrow,
thy pity without end?
O make me thine forever;
and should I fainting be,

Lord, let me never, never
outlive my love for thee.

Why did Jesus suffer so profoundly, yet bring us a message of love and kindness? He, too, like the other great biblical figures ushered in a radical change in society. Jesus specifically turned from the often violent teachings of the Old Testament such as "an eye for an eye," and other accepted behaviors of the society in which he lived. Becoming aware of and developing a deeper understanding concerning the Law of Polarity may provide the insight that we need. If we choose to constantly look for the good in people and situations instead of expecting them to be bad, rude, or whatever other negative trait we often expect from humans, we will find good. "Seek and ye shall find."

The Law of Polarity says that things and situations exist in opposites. We must know what hunger feels like to experience the sated feeling following a meal. We must know what constitutes bad actions in order to know what it means "to be good." So, with this in mind and using the majority of the biblical figures mentioned before, we see that each of the other men I've used as examples had some clearly negative traits in his personality. Yet, all of them, Abraham, Moses, and David, also possessed qualities to find them chosen by God to accomplish great things.

All human beings possess great qualities and negative ones. Look for the good in humans, for that is the example set for us by Jesus. When you find it, tell the person. People love compliments, and the positive idea in your mind makes you feel good. It is often just the polarity event that can raise someone from a state of depression or despair into one of joy and fulfillment. It may be just the act of Christian charity needed to help that person continue on.

A random reading of the scripture one morning led to a great connection for me uniting quantum physics, Christ, and scripture. Several stories relate to Christ healing from a distance, such as John 4:46–54

> 46 *Once more he visited Cana in Galilee, where he had turned the water into wine. And there was a certain royal official whose son lay sick at Capernaum. 47 When this man heard that Jesus had arrived in Galilee from Judea; he went to him and begged him to come and heal his son, who was close to death.*

48 *"Unless you people see miraculous signs and wonders," Jesus told him, "you will never believe."*

49 *The royal official said, "Sir, come down before my child dies."*

50 *Jesus replied, "You may go. Your son will live." The man took Jesus at his word and departed. 51 While he was still on the way, his servants met him with the news that his boy was living. 52 When he inquired as to the time when his son got better, they said to him, "The fever left him yesterday at the seventh hour."*

53 *Then the father realized that this was the exact time at which Jesus had said to him, "Your son will live." So he and all his household believed.*

54 *This was the second miraculous sign that Jesus performed, having come from Judea to Galilee.*

This applies so well to energy as known today as one of the primary rules of quantum physics. Thoughts are also energy. Thoughts are the beginning of manifestation through beliefs. Faith (thought) moves to belief (also thought) and leads to knowing and manifestation of the expected! It may not happen as quickly for those of us just learning to apply these principles. Jesus Christ understood this and could manifest his thoughts in the form of miracles because of his superior grasp of these very basic and simple concepts. Jesus had the benefit of not doubting the power of the Father or the laws. He had the unshakable faith so many of us lack, and quite possibly, it was this that set him apart from "regular" human beings.

Thoughts follow the Law of Gestation and Gender, which tells us that there is a period expected for manifestation. We expect a baby to take nine months to develop, but more and more, we are seeing babies survive and thrive with less of a gestational period. I am not suggesting here, however, that we practice this with the human development. Expected gestational periods provide, in this example, mother, baby, and the entire family the time to become physically prepared for the new addition to the family as well as emotionally and financially, but are the "miracle babies" we see more and more products of simply science or a "new faith" that these "preemies" can survive? It is a curious question to blend science and religion here!

Perhaps this is a similar concept to that of the woman with bleeding. She could be healed by touching Christ's robe. Was this simply her faith in action? She believed. Perhaps Jesus's simple response of "Who touched me?" was from recognition of the total faith he tried desperately to show others. Jesus lacked the ego of most humans, another trait that set him apart. He did not say, "Look how great I am, and I will do it for you every time." He said, "You will do this in my name." That is his gift to us, among many others: that he indeed showed us the way, not only to eternal salvation but to experience the joys and wonders of the natural world via the gift of life on this earth. If we could experience the faith he showed, imagine how much *fun* life would be! Helping others has great rewards. It is one major reason for my career in medicine. I would have changed careers years ago had I felt like I was not helping anyone!

Jesus showed us that we, too, have much to contribute in God's world. He gave us examples. He gave each of us talents that when properly used can make the world a better place. Find your talent. Develop your faith, and share the sheer joy that comes from the realization that faith is the factor for your quantum leap. Miracles happen every day. Jesus showed us how easily they could appear if we just trust and take action.

The story of the woman at the well in John 4: 4–30 is a powerful story related to segregation and its abandonment when you believe in Christ. We're all equal. This scripture is not just meant to hold people living outside the bounds of marriage accountable for the rejection of their vows, but it also shows that the time has come when *what* you are called will not matter nor will *where you go to worship*. It is who you are and the way you live that count before God. Your worship must engage your spirit in the pursuit of truth. Those are types of people the Father is looking for to do His work—those who are simply and honestly behaving as themselves before him in their worship. God is sheer (being energy), or spirit. Those who worship him must do it out of their very being, their spirits, and their true self in adoration. This is how we connect with the divine, which exists in all of us.

46Once more he visited Cana in Galilee, where he had turned the water into wine. And there was a certain royal official whose son lay sick at Capernaum. 47When this man heard that Jesus had arrived in Galilee from Judea, he went to him and begged him to come and heal his son, who was close to death. 48"Unless you people see miraculous signs and wonders," Jesus told him, "you will never believe." 49The royal official said, "Sir, come down before my child dies." 50Jesus replied, "You may go. Your son will live." The man took Jesus at his word and departed. 51While he was still on the way, his servants met him with the news that his boy was living. 52When he inquired as to the time when his son got better, they said to him, "The fever left him yesterday at the seventh hour."

53Then the father realized that this was the exact time at which Jesus had said to him, "Your son will live." So he and all his household believed. 54This was the second miraculous sign that Jesus performed, having come from Judea to Galilee.

–John 4:46–54 (New International Version)

CHAPTER 22

WHAT DO YOU MEAN I'M VIBRATING? I'M SITTING STILL!

> *We make a living by what we get; we make a life by what we give.*
>
> **–Sir Winston Churchill**

Thought is one of the most powerful and potent forms of energy vibrating at one of the highest frequencies. Your thoughts are actually things, as we showed in the previous chapter, and that is one of the reasons that Jesus manifested the miracles he did. He understood the power of thought. The Law of Attraction, which states simply that what we think about is what creates our reality or our life as it is now, is actually a subject within of the Law of Vibration, which states that things that vibrate at similar frequencies attract one another, and things that do not vibrate at the same frequencies repel one another, like the two poles of magnets or oil and water.

The Law of Vibration, which is the basis for the Law of Attraction, states that everything that exists in our universe, whether seen or unseen, broken down into and analyzed in its purest and most basic form, consists of pure energy that resonates and exists as a vibratory frequency or pattern. Again, **everything vibrates; nothing rests.** The Law of Attraction is the universal law that ensures that whatever energy is broadcast out into the universe is joined by (or attracted to) energies that are of an equal or harmonious frequency, resonance, or vibration.

So how do we work with this law without becoming greedy or egotistical? How can this idea, that we have the power to create, work with our spiritual concepts that recognize the Creator as a divine force or God? Is it possible to be healthy, wealthy, and wise and still be a good Christian? Absolutely.

Jack Canfield is the coauthor of the *Chicken Soup for the Soul* series of books that are a publishing phenomenon and some of which many Christians proudly display in their own personal libraries. He has developed a home study course he calls *Dream Big: Living the Law of Attraction*. This course, available on CD and DVD through his company, the Santa Barbara Wellness Institute, breaks down goal writing into several key areas of life. If we look at the areas in life that we wish to focus on and set goals in each, we'll find that our life "works better," and these areas are all those in which we already know Christians should develop in order to live a healthy and wholesome life.

The first area he explains of importance for our lives is financial. Though an archaic mind-set told us that poverty may win us a special place in the kingdom of heaven, do you think Jesus really meant for us to embrace a life of poverty when he told his followers that the poor would always exist, pathetically suffering? I do not. I think he meant we should show compassion for those who cannot find a way to a better financial life. The second area is about having a goal in life, to participate in philanthropy and volunteerism. These areas of focus go hand in hand. If you have more financial abundance or time on your hands, you can *give*.

The third area of focus jives with the first two, and that is to be in a job or career that brings us great satisfaction. If we are happy on the job, we produce more or better results, and the ultimate aim in most careers is to provide a product or service that provides for a better world. I once heard a financial consultant struggle with the idea that his job was so materialistic. When I explained to him that his job helped others earn more with less effort so that their lives were more abundant so that *they* can then share the wealth and blessings, he got a new attitude toward his work and provided better service to his clients who then all made more money off their investments. If thoughts are energy, then so is money, and it is simply the energy that we in this world exchange for the goods and services we need. Money is not bad. Money can and does do great things when it is part of a balanced life, spiritually and financially. In fact, we can say we are "in a relationship with money." Just as there are healthy human relationships, there, too, are healthy relationships with money and investments.

The word *investment* is an interesting concept when applied to human relationships. We do "invest" in them. When you choose a spouse, you invest in your future. Divorce is often a painful awareness of a "failed investment," but failure can be a great teacher. Emotionally unhealthy people often choose the same type of second spouse they chose for a first. We see this often with physical abuse and those suffering from addictions. It's a pattern that repeats. Canfield shows us that personal relationships are another area that we should pay careful attention to in our lives. Miracles in the healing of relationships occur frequently if we are the instrument of love and forgiveness through which God can send the healing. So this fourth category is an area we may actually want to set goals in. Perhaps you want to heal that long-standing feud with your brother or ex-spouse.

The best way to begin that process is to "be the change you want to see in the world" as the late Mohandas Gandhi said. Start by doing what you can, which you already are by simply reading this book, and "get right" with yourself spiritually. Accomplish those things you wanted to whether it is to study under a specific teacher, read the Bible in its entirety in a year, teach a Bible study course, or earn a degree, and as you begin to feel good about yourself, you will heal that within you (with God's help) to enable you to reach out and begin repairing those broken lines of love that are our relationships. Since we cannot control others, the only way to heal a damaged friendship or love relationship is to be the best you can be, pray, and have faith, and then take the initial step toward mending. With true intention and faith, miraculous healing in seemingly impossible situations can occur.

Though it is neither the most important nor the least important area of your life for goal setting, set goals to strive for better health each day. Take good care of the body temple that God has blessed you with. If you feel it is vain to strive for a goal weight, consult a medical professional and get an educated opinion on what is the healthiest weight for you. Exercise. Nothing can replace exercise. Eat with care but enjoy the abundance of God's creation—food. When we have healthy bodies, we can focus more clearly, we have more physical stamina, and our emotions are easier to control. It is vital that all seven areas are in balance, for with healthy goals in each area, which we write down and visit daily, our lives begin to work more efficiently. It's like having a tune-up on your automobile. It just works better when we get all of the parts operating at peak performance.

> [11]*In him we were also chosen, having been predestined according to the plan of him who works out everything in conformity with the purpose of his will,*
>
> **–Ephesians 1:11 (New International Version)**

CHAPTER 23

THE EVOLUTION OF FAITH

> *Obstacles are the frightful things you see when you take your eyes off your goals.*
>
> **–Henry Ford**

Ask even the most schooled theologians to define faith, and they'll likely give you a definition in contrast to doubt and based upon the accepted dogma and doctrine within that denomination. But is doubt the right word? I think the contrast is better summed up as belief versus nonbelief. Faith is often put forth as a system of religious beliefs. We may have a creed stated or we "believe what we're told." But faith is an extension beyond normal belief—as in "I believe if I drop the apple, it will fall." That is a belief you have that can be proven. Faith is yet a step beyond into the reality of the unproven and further into those things that can never be proven.

Some good examples would be the belief in centuries past that the earth was the center of the universe. While this was eventually proven false, that didn't lessen the faith of those who did believe this to be true in the fifteenth century—to the point they were ready to persecute those who suggested otherwise.

In some religious circles, if you appear skeptical of a particular idea, you may be told that you lack faith. This accusation that you may be less than devout has kept some religious ideas in practice that were never useful to those seeking God in the first place. It intimates that there is one correct way to faith, and all others are less than and to seek answers is somehow offensive to God.

Augustine of Hippo, Bishop of Alexandria, spent much of his early life seeking God and actually explored some concepts outside the orthodox Christianity of his time, specifically Manichaeism, whose principles teach the duality between good and evil. During this phase, he diligently worked at trying to prove there is a God. He also became very involved in neoplatonism, which emphasized the mind's participation in divine light, beauty, and goodness. It was only when he went to Milan as a professor that he experienced a mystical conversion to Christianity, inspired from the teachings of Ambrose in 386 at the age of 32 and formed a semimonastic community. From this point in his life, he rose to the status of an authoritative figure within the early Christian Church. What he arrived at in his mission was the idea that "faith is a verb." It is an action word. You have to believe in God and have faith that God will provide. It is an assurance, an underlying knowing that permeates your life, not a ritual you perform or a set of rules you follow.

Most Americans remember the shock and horror of the September 11, 2001, attacks by Islamic terrorists. What those terrorists did that day was a matter of faith. They gave their lives to support a cause in which they truly believed with unwavering faith. As a medical doctor, I find it hard to believe that a human being could not only be willing to take his own life in such a manner, but to also take the lives of so many along with them. It is incomprehensible to me, and I've seen the horrors of war. The *survival instinct* seems to have been overcome in that situation by faith. They truly believed that they were doing the will of God and sought paradise for a cause in which they would never know the final outcome. And if indeed this was done by faith, how then can we turn faith into a positive? This is an extreme and somber example of the power of faith.

Faith can be life enhancing and a powerful force for good in our lives when we use it to support who we are and not who others say we should be. The example used of the Islamic terrorists show men who believed in a cause that very likely was created and taught to them by others in whom they placed their faith. This is, in my opinion, misdirected faith. Trust yourself, trust God, and most importantly, trust your conscience. You are a person. You have the capacity to think and should do so for yourself. What is appropriate for your neighbor may not be in your best interest. This is especially difficult when we compare ourselves to family members because, surely, relatives all share complementary values, right? Not necessarily.

You are an individual. You may have to make decisions for a group such as your family or your employees or staff, but most of our decisions are for ourselves and should stem from a place of inner confidence. But sometimes nonbelief creeps in. Fear grips us during some routine or seemingly harmless process of decision making. What if I make this investment and it does not bring a return? What if I lose this client because he is not happy with the product or service? Does this show a lack of faith?

Perhaps a better way to look at these moments is that they help us make an informed decision. We ask questions. Often we can find the answers from those we trust or experts, but just as often we cannot. Whether it is buying a new pair of shoes or committing to a person for the rest of your life, you often resort to faith for the decisions you make whether you know it or not. We have "gut feelings" and instincts that often prove beneficial in our decision-making process. Some people never seem to face any doubts and appear to move forward in every moment of their life without much holding them back, while others allow fear and uncertainty to plague their every move.

Beware of allowing fear to overwhelm your thoughts. Manage them. Ask yourself, "Is this a rational fear? What would happen if I chose the wrong thing? Would I fail? And is failure really failure in this case, or is it simply redirection?" Many of us look back on our lives and see that those events, relationships, and circumstances we thought of as failures in the moment were actually a redirection. A divine guidance, perhaps, took us down another path along which life became grander and happier than we could have ever imagined.

No human has escaped the experience of failure. We all reflect and have moments of pride and moments of shame. In fact, they are the opposite of each experience, and in the field of quantum physics, we see this as the Law of Relativity and also as the Law of Polarity. We understand things in relation to something else as in the former and to its opposite in the latter. Therefore, because we fear making the wrong decision, this does not show a lack of faith until it begins to incapacitate you and prevent you from making a decision at all.

You are a person first, with God-given abilities to think. First put your thoughts in the positive because whenever we look at our desires in the negative, the negative is what we manifest. Think of any situation that persists in your life. Do you feel you need to lose a lot of weight? Do you say to yourself, "I'm tired of being fat!" or "I don't want to be fat"? If you phrase any situation, whether it be health, wealth ("I don't want to be broke"), or relationships ("I wish I wasn't so miserable in my marriage"), in a way similar to any of these statements, you're focusing on the negative. You are placing your faith in the direction of the negatives in your life.

Instead, say to yourself, "I weigh (and state your goal weight)." Look at yourself in the mirror and look for the beauty in your face. Ignore the wrinkles, blemishes, or whatever you dislike and find that one feature you love. Then tell yourself you are beautiful.

This is very difficult to do with ourselves and easy to do with some other humans such as babies and children. We look at even the most physically deformed children and see beauty, yet when it comes to ourselves or, unfortunately, our spouses, we often focus on the negative aspects of their form or personality. Try finding one thing about your spouse or children if this is an issue for you, that you love and adore. Focus on that. Instead of saying, "My children are slobs, and I wish they'd pick up after themselves," find the qualities you adore in them and remind yourself of them. Then tell *them*.

Remind your children, spouse, or coworkers often of the qualities they have that are wonderful. You'll soon find that they do more of those good things and fewer of the ones that irk you so much. Or is it simply a new perspective? Did they change because you pointed out their good qualities? Did you change because you're now in a state of gratitude for who they are instead of constantly griping about what a chore it is to deal with that person—that person you love so much? Is it that both parties are evolving? Even your spouse to whom you've become so accustomed, or your business partner with whom you've been in business for 35 years and can predict his movements to the second, is evolving.

Everyone is changing. Change with them. Flow with them in your own dance, for to resist is go contrary to the natural forces established by God that operate our world and the entire universe. You wouldn't dare try to resist the force of gravity. When we look for good, we find it. When we look for bad, we find it. Why not choose to look for the good? Gratitude can change your life.

So I begin this chapter with faith and end with gratitude. What does gratitude have to do with faith? Everything. In being grateful, we attract more to be grateful for. Things work easier in our lives, whether it is our relationships, our finances, or our health. When we are in that state, we see more and more things for which to be grateful, and then it snowballs. The goodness and abundance comes in from everywhere, making the bumps on the road of life so much easier to traverse. And it all started by taking a leap of faith. We are willing to make choices and decisions that get us moving, and so long as we feel we are moving in the right direction, God tends to show us how we are doing by what appears in our life. So appreciate what he has sent to you, and you'll find he will send you even more. Be a leader in faith and gratitude, for leadership is a force of faith. Leaders think of infinite possibilities, and they do it by focusing on the potential in all people and situations. Good leaders find things for which to be grateful, that is, the strengths of those they lead, to best utilize.

Love

[1]If I speak in the tongues[j] of men and of angels, but have not love, I am only a resounding gong or a clanging cymbal. [2]If I have the gift of prophecy and can fathom all mysteries and all knowledge, and if I have a faith that can move mountains, but have not love, I am nothing. [3]If I give all I possess to the poor and surrender my body to the flames, but have not love, I gain nothing.

[4]Love is patient, love is kind. It does not envy, it does not boast, it is not proud. [5]It is not rude, it is not self-seeking, it is not easily angered, it keeps no record of wrongs. [6]Love does not delight in evil but rejoices with the truth. [7]It always protects, always trusts, always hopes, always perseveres.

[8]Love never fails. But where there are prophecies, they will cease; where there are tongues, they will be stilled; where there is knowledge, it will pass away. [9]For we know in part and we prophesy in part, [10]but when perfection comes, the imperfect disappears. [11]When I was a child, I talked like a child, I thought like a child, I reasoned like a child. When I became a man, I put childish ways behind me. [12]Now we see but a poor reflection as in a mirror; then we shall see face to face. Now I know in part; then I shall know fully, even as I am fully known.

[13]And now these three remain: faith, hope and love. But the greatest of these is love.

–1 Corinthians 13 (New International Version)

CHAPTER 24

CARING FOR YOUR CONSCIOUSNESS

Do not follow where the path may lead, go instead where there is no path and leave a trail.

–Ralph Waldo Emerson

Have you ever contemplated your conscious thoughts and the impact they have on your day, the experience of those around you, or even your health? Caring for your consciousness is vital. Conscious awareness of vibration is called *feeling*. When we are aware of our thoughts, whether negative or positive, we can change or adjust them. Your thoughts control your emotions and paradigms, your perception of yourself, your life, and what you deserve, and it also controls your vibration, which dictates what you attract. Happy, joyous thoughts may be just the medicine for a bad day, but this not done at the expense of dealing with reality, either.

Paying bills is a good example of a stress we all face no matter what our income level is, for as income increases, we often find our expenses increase along with it. If you find that this is a stressful process, it is not prudent to put it off in lieu of happier thoughts of romping in the surf on the ideal vacation. But facing them without fear or in a state of feeling lack and scarcity is a choice. Being responsible in the process to deal with each creditor or bill will produce more desirable results, even if you do not have, at the moment, enough funds to pay each one. Arm yourself in this instance with an updated bank statement—most are available updated daily online—a good calculator, a quiet place, and a peaceful mind. We must face our fears, and often we find it is not as frightening as we imagined, but failing to do so will produce unintended outcomes. It is very easy to see this if we simply neglect our bills, even for a month. You may find yourself sitting in the dark without running water and the niceties of life.

This is also the case if you find yourself having to deal with a person who has caused you harm, taken advantage of another, or someone whose behavior has become unacceptable in some way where you must now set some boundaries. We find this often in families. Obsessing on the horrible or perceived atrocious actions of a person or the injustice you've seen or felt is not a way to go into such a situation in order to achieve any desirable results nor is avoidance. But how do we get to that place of peace in order to take action that will give us the results we desire or even results that exceed our expectations in a positive way?

When you are not feeling well emotionally or physically, find yourself dwelling on feelings of anger, hatred, or fear, become aware of what you are thinking, and then think of something pleasant. If, for example, you're facing an issue with another person and have dwelled only on the injustice, think of something good and wonderful about that person. If you're facing financial dilemmas, find the abundance you have in your life—you may have a pantry full of food or a closet full of clothes you no longer wear.

It's a funny phenomenon, but if we're facing financial woes, sometimes it is a great practice to unload a closet and give some things to a charitable organization, donate some canned goods to a food drive, or go out and help someone in a way that costs you nothing. Help your neighbor sweep his drive after mowing, help someone carry packages or wash their car. Write a letter or email to someone you know may be thrilled to hear from you, or from anyone. These acts of giving put us in a great state of mind for facing the issues we must face.

In addition to thoughts and action to put us in a better frame of mind, I would like to discuss the importance of monitoring your thoughts daily, whether through daily quiet time or meditation or whatever form it takes for you. This is when we clear our minds in order to let the communication from God come to us. It is often when we receive the solutions to the dilemmas we face.

Sometimes exercises in mental discipline, such as training your mind to think a certain way or entertain more positive versus negative thoughts, is an aim of some types of consciousness control. By focusing on one object, such as a river, a tree, or a waterfall, and being conscious of where you are, you can allow your mind to be freed from the noise of life. John Assaraf, in *The Power of Meditation*, tells us that this type of exercise and "meditative practices change the workings of the brain and allow people to achieve different levels of awareness." By doing this, you will find that you also reach another level of peace. Human beings strive for different things, so peace for one person may not be the same state of awareness for another. It's a personal journey to find the best level of tranquility or peace for you at this time in your life. Perhaps even for this moment in your life.

By improving one's life through the conscious control of thought, we see a reduction in anxiety and depression, which will improve relationships and health. Studies have also confirmed an ancient belief that those who are capable of more sustained meditation experiences actually require less sleep. While this is against sound medical advice, there is no doubt that the ability to clear the mind, and thus induce a state of calm restfulness, adds to the body's ability to recuperate from the stresses and strains of life.

By sitting quietly in a calm and relaxed environment and consciously clearing the mind, you allow the brain to release the worries and fears you may be harboring over seemingly insignificant events. Most of us don't realize all these little incidents and actions throughout the day are cumulative, and by not taking time to clear the conscious mind, we inadvertently dwell on minutia rather than focusing on our goals.

Each time a disturbing thought enters your mind, clear it. This will take practice, but with time, you'll find it easier and easier to extend the periods when your mind is free of the clutter and chatter that occupy your thoughts. Pave the way for the Lord to speak to you in your quiet time. Give your mind and your body time to relax and restore themselves. Then go take on your day, especially if it includes paying the bills or resolving the issues with your estranged brother.

[31] *To the Jews who had believed him, Jesus said, "If you hold to my teaching, you are really my disciples.* [32] *Then you will know the truth, and the truth will set you free."*

–John 8:31–32 (New International Version)

[1] *Therefore, holy brothers, who share in the heavenly calling, fix your thoughts on Jesus, the apostle and high priest whom we confess.* [2] *He was faithful to the one who appointed him, just as Moses was faithful in all God's house.* [3] *Jesus has been found worthy of greater honor than Moses, just as the builder of a house has greater honor than the house itself.* [4] *For every house is built by someone, but God is the builder of everything.* [5] *Moses was faithful as a servant in all God's house, testifying to what would be said in the future.* [6] *But Christ is faithful as a son over God's house. And we are his house, if we hold on to our courage and the hope of which we boast.*

[7]So, as the Holy Spirit says: "Today, if you hear his voice, [8]do not harden your hearts
as you did in the rebellion, during the time of testing in the desert, [9]where your fathers tested and tried me and for forty years saw what I did. [10]That is why I was angry with that generation, and I said, 'Their hearts are always going astray, and they have not known my ways."
[11]So I declared on oath in my anger, "They shall never enter my rest."

–Hebrews 3:1–11 (New International Version)

CHAPTER 25

LAW OF CAUSE AND EFFECT

People don't care how much you know until they know how much you care.

–John C. Maxwell

Cause and effect is a concept often used in all types of persuasive writing and storytelling that links situations and events together in time, with causes preceding effects. But causation involves more than sequence: cause-and-effect analysis explains why something happened—or is happening—and it predicts what will likely occur. Sometimes many different causes can be responsible for one effect. Sometimes one cause will have several effects, such as when we break a glass, the pieces shatter and may at the same time scratch the floor or cause a wound to someone. A single gunshot can penetrate two human beings on occasion. Cross words to a spouse in front of a child can hurt your spouse and your child.

Physics tells us that every action has an equal and opposite reaction. Every cause must have an effect. Anything that is a cause is actually the effect of something that came before it, and the effect becomes the cause of something else. Nothing in this world means nothing or is without repercussions. Some results are good or even fantastic while others may be not so desirable. Why is it that we want to take credit for a job well done, such as the creation of a work of art, yet if our life is in shambles with our relationships in turmoil, our finances out of control, and our health not in the ideal condition we want, we often hear, "It's not *my* fault"?

Our lives are products of our choices, which are first thoughts. Our thoughts cause our feelings and actions. It is rare to make a decision without first giving it at least a few seconds of thought, or so we thought! Each thought leads to actions that will have a reaction, and it continues on infinitely. It is impossible to start a new chain of events. This law shows us the universe is a perpetual, never-ending cycle. What are you doing that is creating your own life's ups and downs? Learn to look at how you create your own good times, give thanks, and do more of those things.

Research has shown that the subconscious mind processes a decision about ten seconds before the conscious mind makes it. That's interesting because it says we already "know" what decisions we are going to make before we decide. It is for this reason that it is imperative that we practice only good thoughts and pure states of operating. For our subconscious mind is so deeply trained in our normal, though often dysfunctional, behavior that when we retrain the mind, we have to go deeper than our thoughts. This is a very nice effect of meditation and mind techniques designed to help you choose conscious thoughts more carefully.

We've been trained to look at the symptoms in our lives. This is not just a practice of physicians. We all do it. We're looking for the effect. A runny nose often prompts the ingestion of antihistamines. A fever is treated with acetaminophen or ibuprofen. But what are these really signaling? They are telling us there is an infection. Is it really wise to just eradicate the symptom without first at least examining the cause? We do this because we've been conditioned to do so. Change is difficult, but change is always happening.

Symptoms in our emotional lives are often spiritual messages about why we're here and who we are. We must get to the root or cause of the problem that produces the symptom, and so often it's much more deeply entrenched in the spiritual "body" before manifesting in the physical form as disease. More and more researchers are seeing the physiological effects of spiritual and emotional causes, and Bruce Lipton tells us, "Only when Spirit and Science are reunited will we be afforded the means to create a better world." As we learned in earlier chapters, the two were once united, but, Lipton explains, "There was a time when it was necessary for scientists to split from Spirit, or at least the corruption of the Spirit by the Church. This powerful institution was in the business of suppressing scientific discovery when it was at odds with Church dogma." So science created its own place in the world apart from the control of the church. It had to split to make any progress. So now the pendulum is swinging back to a place where more and more scientists are publishing on the idea of combining science and religion and spirituality.

There is no doubt that doing good deeds, tithing, ministering to others, and all the ways we are taught to be good Christians has a physiological benefit for us. That's wonderful, but how can we affect the lives of other people by a shift in our beliefs? You are the epicenter of change. Be the change you want to see. If you'd like to see an end to gossip in your personal groups, stop it in progress. Find something positive to say about the person or people being gossiped about, for example. This has a great effect on killing the conversation. You'll soon find that others won't do it around you, and it will become less acceptable to see this type of behavior in your social circles. But you *be the one* to start. Lead by example. Robert Williams, teaches us to "tithe only to the light and that will grow. Look only for the light in people." In other words, only focus on the good in people, even if it is really hard to find that tiny spark of goodness. When we find it and acknowledge it, their goodness has a path to travel and grow. They do still have free will, but your acknowledgment of their good, the divine in them, will come through when we call to it.

I'd like to end this chapter with a story from the book of Esther, showing how a simple act can cause miraculous effects. In the story, the servant of Naaman's wife, a girl not mentioned by name, tells her mistress that the leprosy Naaman suffered with could be cured by the prophet Elisha. Naaman tries to handle this by asking his king (of Syria) to implore the king of Israel. The king of Israel is upset, as he knows he can't cure leprosy and is convinced it is a plot by the Syrians. Elisha hears of this issue and sends word to the man to come and see him. The man does and is given the simple instructions, "Wash yourself seven times in the Jordan River." Naaman is cured, and the greatness of God is acknowledged by a huge audience. All from the willingness of one simple girl to speak out when she knew some way to help her master, though she had every reason not to. We all have that power. We all have something to give. Find your spark and have it light the way for others, for like all good things, it will come back to you, just as the tide comes in and goes out every day.

Naaman Healed of Leprosy

[1] Now Naaman was commander of the army of the king of Aram. He was a great man in the sight of his master and highly regarded, because through him the LORD had given victory to Aram. He was a valiant soldier, but he had leprosy. [2] Now bands from Aram had gone out and had taken captive a young girl from Israel, and she served Naaman's wife. [3] She said to her mistress, "If only my master would see the prophet who is in Samaria! He would cure him of his leprosy."

[4] Naaman went to his master and told him what the girl from Israel had said. [5] "By all means, go," the king of Aram replied. "I will send a letter to the king of Israel." So Naaman left, taking with him ten talents [b] of silver, six thousand shekels [c] of gold and ten sets of clothing. [6] The letter that he took to the king of Israel read: "With this letter I am sending my servant Naaman to you so that you may cure him of his leprosy." [7] As soon as the king of Israel read the letter, he tore his robes and said, "Am I God? Can I kill and bring back to life? Why does this fellow send someone to me to be cured of his leprosy?

See how he is trying to pick a quarrel with me!" [8] *When Elisha the man of God heard that the king of Israel had torn his robes, he sent him this message: "Why have you torn your robes? Have the man come to me and he will know that there is a prophet in Israel."* [9] *So Naaman went with his horses and chariots and stopped at the door of Elisha's house.* [10] *Elisha sent a messenger to say to him, "Go, wash yourself seven times in the Jordan, and your flesh will be restored and you will be cleansed."* [11] *But Naaman went away angry and said, "I thought that he would surely come out to me and stand and call on the name of the LORD his God, wave his hand over the spot and cure me of my leprosy.* [12] *Are not Abana and Pharpar, the rivers of Damascus, better than any of the waters of Israel? Couldn't I wash in them and be cleansed?" So he turned and went off in a rage.*

[13] *Naaman's servants went to him and said, "My father, if the prophet had told you to do some great thing, would you not have done it? How much more, then, when he tells you, 'Wash and be cleansed'!"* [14] *So he went down and dipped himself in the Jordan seven times, as the*

man of God had told him, and his flesh was restored and became clean like that of a young boy.

[15] Then Naaman and all his attendants went back to the man of God. He stood before him and said, "Now I know that there is no God in all the world except in Israel. Please accept now a gift from your servant." [16] The prophet answered, "As surely as the LORD lives, whom I serve, I will not accept a thing." And even though Naaman urged him, he refused. [17] "If you will not," said Naaman, "please let me, your servant, be given as much earth as a pair of mules can carry, for your servant will never again make burnt offerings and sacrifices to any other god but the LORD. [18] But may the LORD forgive your servant for this one thing: When my master enters the temple of Rimmon to bow down and he is leaning on my arm and I bow there also—when I bow down in the temple of Rimmon, may the LORD forgive your servant for this." [19] "Go in peace," Elisha said. After Naaman had traveled some distance, [20] Gehazi, the servant of Elisha the man of God, said to himself, "My master was too easy on Naaman, this Aramean, by not accepting

from him what he brought. As surely as the LORD lives,
I will run after him and get something from him." ²¹
So Gehazi hurried after Naaman. When Naaman saw
him running toward him, he got down from the chariot
to meet him. "Is everything all right?" he asked. ²²
"Everything is all right," Gehazi answered. "My master
sent me to say, 'Two young men from the company of the
prophets have just come to me from the hill country of
Ephraim. Please give them a talent [d] *of silver and two*
sets of clothing.' "

²³ *"By all means, take two talents," said Naaman. He*
urged Gehazi to accept them, and then tied up the two
talents of silver in two bags, with two sets of clothing. He
gave them to two of his servants, and they carried them
ahead of Gehazi.

–2 Kings 5:1–23 (New International Version)

²⁷And there were many in Israel with leprosy[a] in the time of Elisha the prophet, yet not one of them was cleansed—only Naaman the Syrian."

²⁸All the people in the synagogue were furious when they heard this. ²⁹They got up, drove him out of the town, and took him to the brow of the hill on which the town was built, in order to throw him down the cliff. ³⁰But he walked right through the crowd and went on his way.

³¹Then he went down to Capernaum, a town in Galilee, and on the Sabbath began to teach the people. ³²They were amazed at his teaching, because his message had authority.

–Luke 4:27–32 (New International Version)

CHAPTER 26

PRAISE FOR THE SOURCE OF ALL CREATION

Nothing great was ever achieved without enthusiasm (God within).

–Ralph Waldo Emerson

129. Give to the Winds Thy Fears

Text: Paul Gerhardt; trans. by John Wesley
Music: William H. Walter
Tune: FESTAL SONG, *Meter:* SM

1. Give to the winds thy fears;
hope and be undismayed.
God hears thy sighs and counts thy tears,
God shall lift up thy head.

2. Through waves and clouds and storms,
God gently clears the way;
wait thou God's time; so shall this night
soon end in joyous day.

3. Leave to God's sovereign sway
to choose and to command;
so shalt thou, wondering, own that way,
how wise, how strong this hand.

4. Let us in life, in death,
thy steadfast truth declare,
and publish with our latest breath
thy love and guardian care.

The Law of Rhythm states that there is a rhythm to life that keeps us flowing as it does all of nature. For example, the tide goes out and comes in because night follows day (the gravitational pull of the moon, which is brought into "view" by the rotation of the earth, causes high and low tide in a never-ending cycle. In the same way, good times follow bad times if we allow ourselves to grow from the experience. When you are on a downswing, do not feel bad. Know this state is temporary; the swing will change and things will get better. There are good times coming—

think of them. We must all feel joy and sorrow, experience abundance and struggle, for these life experiences are what enable us to grow as humans.

Ecclesiastes acknowledges this law with the following passage:

1. There is an appointed time for everything. And there is a time for every event under heaven—

2. A time to give birth and a time to die; A time to plant and a time to uproot what is planted.

3. A time to kill and a time to heal; A time to tear down and a time to build up.

4. A time to weep and a time to laugh; A time to mourn and a time to dance.

5. A time to throw stones and a time to gather stones; A time to embrace and a time to shun embracing.

6. A time to search and a time to give up as lost; A time to keep and a time to throw away.

7. A time to tear apart and a time to sew together; A time to be silent and a time to speak.

8. A time to love and a time to hate; A time for war and a time for peace.

9. What profit is there to the worker from that in which he toils?

10. I have seen the task which God has given the sons of men with which to occupy themselves.

(New American Standard Bible)

The comfort of this passage is the acknowledgment that there is a pattern to life. We are not surrounded by unexplained randomness. The same is true in the scientific realm. There are patterns and flow to everything, from the smallest atom to the vastness of the galaxies we know—and even those yet to be discovered. It is comforting due to the idea that no event or circumstance in life can ruin our futures unless we allow it to. Life will return to normal, and the sun will come up again, each day providing us new opportunities and experiences.

It is common for some people to take an all or nothing approach to their lives, which means they have extreme highs and lows. They bounce from extreme excitement to extreme disappointment when things don't work out according to the way they initially perceive the way things should go. It is important to understand that much of their emotional state is due to their emotions, not the circumstances themselves. Jobs come and go, possessions come and go, even relationships come and go.

The Law of Rhythm holds true that your life will continue no matter how devastated you may feel at the moment. This gives us hope for the future and the assurance that we can try again, or start over, to improve our lives. The worst thing you can do is refuse to move forward. This is because there is no such thing as maintaining the status quo. Life is always moving forward; you don't have the power to stop it, just as you can't stop the tide from coming in or going out. To think that you can remain as you are right now is just a delusion—none of us ever remain the same, and even if we could, those around us would continue to change.

I frequently hear people, especially those in the church, lament that things are always changing for the worse. I argue that this is their perception. Yes things always change, but are they really worse? We live in a fabulous age of technological advances that allow you to stand in the sand next to the great pyramids of Egypt and speak to another person half way around the world. We are more knowledgeable and able to focus on personal growth through the lessons of others. All of these are good things.

One point of note is that many of the items we perceive to be worse are the same things that have happened for centuries. Wars, murders, and crimes against innocents have all occurred as long as there have been people on the earth. Cain killed his own brother Abel in the first biblically documented murder. The difference between then and now is that we all know about all the bad, destructive, and horrific acts that go on every day as they are broadcast into our living rooms every night or posted on the Internet.

Know that these things are part of our world but are not an excuse for you to dwell on them to the point it keeps you from moving forward. Even when things are bad, they will improve again, and if you know that fact and believe it, you will be much more able to weather any storm life throws your way.

A Time for Everything

[1] *There is a time for everything, and a season for every activity under heaven:*

[2] *a time to be born and a time to die, a time to plant and a time to uproot,*

[3] *a time to kill and a time to heal, a time to tear down and a time to build,*

[4] *a time to weep and a time to laugh, a time to mourn and a time to dance,*

[5] *a time to scatter stones and a time to gather them, a time to embrace and a time to refrain,*

[6] *a time to search and a time to give up, a time to keep and a time to throw away,*

[7] *a time to tear and a time to mend, a time to be silent and a time to speak,*

[8] *a time to love and a time to hate, a time for war and a time for peace.*

–Ecclesiastes 3:1–8 (New International Version)

CHAPTER 27

SOW I SHALL REAP?

> *In the middle of difficulty lies opportunity.*
>
> **–Albert Einstein**

One of the hardest laws for people to really grasp is the idea of the Law of Gestation and Gender. This law states that everything—every being, plant organism, and every idea—has an incubation period. The idea that things take time is a source of frustration for many, as they want to have an idea instantly manifest in their lives. It does not work that way and can only manifest after an incubation period when the time is right. It is very much as if you plant a flower seed in the winter. The cold will keep the seed dormant until the right mix of water, warmth, and sunlight are available. It is then, and only then, that the seed will grow.

One area that this law is often applied to is the area of goal setting. For example, if you decide you want to become a real-estate mogul but are currently a school teacher, then the idea will only come into being as you seek knowledge about real estate and meet people who can mentor and help you. Only then will you be on the way to meeting your goal.

There are false assumptions concerning the Law of Gestation and Gender that can confuse people as well. Some think that because there is an incubation period, they should sit on the couch at home and not do anything because they have no control over the timing. This is untrue. As you step on the path to your goal or desires, those people and things you need to accomplish it will come to you. However, if you never take that step, it will merely remain an idea.

You can think back to the seed. If you buy a packet of seeds and leave them in a drawer in your house, no plant will ever grow. That seed must be in the environment to get the nourishment it needs. Similarly, your goals and ideas should be given a rich environment in which to develop. If you want to pursue great personal growth, you should frequently be around others who have experienced such growth to get the guidance and help you need. If your goal is to attain financial security for your family, you should seek the knowledge and fellowship of others who have created financial security for their families. Whatever your desire, the Law of Gestation and Gender is working to help your ideas come to fruition, but you bear some responsibility to put yourself in a suitable environment.

The Bible addresses the Law of Gestation and Gender with the following scripture:

⁶ One who is taught the word must share all good things with the one who teaches. ⁷ Do not be deceived: God is not mocked, for whatever one sows, that will he also reap. ⁸For the one who sows to his own flesh will from the flesh reap corruption, but the one who sows to the Spirit will from the Spirit reap eternal life. ⁹And let us not grow weary of doing good, for in due season we will reap, if we do not give up. ¹⁰So then, as we have opportunity, let us do good to everyone, and especially to those who are of the household of faith.

–Galatians 6:6–18 (English Standard Version)

This passage points out another aspect of the Law of Gestation and Gender that people can misunderstand, and that is the idea that you can't improve your life if you never strive to. You may hear people complain on occasion that they tried to improve their lives and set certain goals, and it didn't work. But often, they did not put themselves in an environment that was conducive to meeting that goal. They got impatient and gave up, rather than allowing the idea to take form and manifest in their lives.

Verse 7 contains a stern warning: "Do not be deceived: God is not mocked, for whatever one sows, that will he also reap." This warning is so that you will not deceive yourself into believing you have given something a try when in reality, you quit. It is an admonishment that you cannot delude yourself into blaming God, the universe, or anyone other than yourself for your results.

If you are constantly working toward your goals, you are sowing just as a farmer plants a field. He does not just plant one grain; he plants many, and so should you. While it may feel like you are giving and giving and doing and doing, in reality you are planting the seeds of your success. One of the interesting books I've read lately is *The Tipping Point* by Malcolm Gladwell about how word of mouth works. His assertion is that it takes a great deal of work and effort, but at some point (the tipping point), all of that effort will take on a life of its own and become self-fulfilling. This is the Law of Gestation and Gender at work. You sow repeatedly and often and when the idea is ready to germinate it takes off on its own and explodes into a full manifestation that reflects all the work you have put in.

When we look at the life of Jesus, we see him constantly sowing. He wasn't teaching thousands at a time and drawing large crowds. He made small, yet constant effort within the fertile hearts that were ready to receive his ideas. Because those seeds were cultivated over time, Christianity survived relentless persecution over centuries.

As you sow the seeds of success and happiness in your own life, know that it is a process that will bear fruit in your future, and the actions you take today will determine how that dream or goal manifests.

⁶Anyone who receives instruction in the word must share all good things with his instructor. ⁷Do not be deceived: God cannot be mocked. A man reaps what he sows. ⁸The one who sows to please his sinful nature, from that nature will reap destruction; the one who sows to please the Spirit, from the Spirit will reap eternal life. ⁹Let us not become weary in doing good, for at the proper time we will reap a harvest if we do not give up. ¹⁰Therefore, as we have opportunity, let us do good to all people, especially to those who belong to the family of believers. ¹¹See what large letters I use as I write to you with my own hand! ¹²Those who want to make a good impression outwardly are trying to compel you to be circumcised. The only reason they do this is to avoid being persecuted for the cross of Christ. [13]Not even those who are circumcised obey the law, yet they want you to be circumcised that they may boast about your flesh. [14]May I never boast except in the cross of our Lord Jesus Christ, through which the world has been crucified to me, and I to the world. [15]Neither circumcision nor uncircumcision means anything; what counts is a new creation. [16]Peace and mercy to all who follow this rule, even to the Israel of God. [17]Finally, let no one cause me trouble, for I bear on my body the marks of Jesus. [18]The grace of our Lord Jesus Christ be with your spirit, brothers. Amen.

–Galatians 6:6–18 (New International Version)

CHAPTER 28

MOSES: TEN TRIES WITH GOD'S HELP!

Nearly all men can understand adversity, but if you want to test a man's character, give him power.

–Abraham Lincoln

If the Law of Gestation and Gender states that which you sow, you reap, then what if you make mistakes or what if things don't seem to go your way, even though you tried your best? Moses is a great example of what can and will go wrong on occasion. Though it is interesting to note that even the seeming failures of Moses were creating the environment for eventual success.

Moses was given the objective to free the Israelites from Pharaoh's grip of slavery. His first request of Pharaoh was to allow the Israelites to attend a festival in the desert in God's honor. One of the reasons that I find these passages so intriguing is that they are a virtual blow by blow between Moses and Pharaoh. It is interesting how long Pharaoh held out and refused to grant Moses's request, even in the face of great suffering upon the land of Egypt.

Exodus 5

Bricks without Straw

1 *Afterward Moses and Aaron went to Pharaoh and said, "This is what the LORD, the God of Israel, says: 'Let my people go, so that they may hold a festival to me in the desert.'"*

2 *Pharaoh said, "Who is the LORD, that I should obey him and let Israel go? I do not know the LORD and I will not let Israel go."*

3 *Then they said, "The God of the Hebrews has met with us. Now let us take a three-day journey into the desert to offer sacrifices to the LORD our God, or he may strike us with plagues or with the sword."*

4 *But the king of Egypt said, "Moses and Aaron, why are you taking the people away from their labor? Get back to*

your work!" 5 Then Pharaoh said, "Look, the people of the land are now numerous, and you are stopping them from working."

6 That same day Pharaoh gave this order to the slave drivers and foremen in charge of the people: 7 "You are no longer to supply the people with straw for making bricks; let them go and gather their own straw. 8 But require them to make the same number of bricks as before; don't reduce the quota. They are lazy; that is why they are crying out, 'Let us go and sacrifice to our God.' 9 Make the work harder for the men so that they keep working and pay no attention to lies."

10 Then the slave drivers and the foremen went out and said to the people, "This is what Pharaoh says: 'I will not give you any more straw. 11 Go and get your own straw wherever you can find it, but your work will not be reduced at all.'" 12 So the people scattered all over Egypt to gather stubble to use for straw. 13 The slave drivers kept pressing them, saying, "Complete the work required of you for each day, just as when you had straw." 14 The Israelite foremen appointed by Pharaoh's slave drivers were beaten and were asked, "Why didn't you meet your quota of bricks yesterday or today, as before?"

15 Then the Israelite foremen went and appealed to Pharaoh: "Why have you treated your servants this way? 16 Your servants are given no straw, yet we are told, 'Make bricks!' Your servants are being beaten, but the fault is with your own people."

17 Pharaoh said, "Lazy, that's what you are—lazy! That is why you keep saying, 'Let us go and sacrifice to

the LORD.' 18 Now get to work. You will not be given
any straw, yet you must produce your full quota
of bricks."

19 The Israelite foremen realized they were in trouble
when they were told, "You are not to reduce the number
of bricks required of you for each day." 20 When they left
Pharaoh, they found Moses and Aaron waiting to meet
them, 21 and they said, "May the LORD look upon you
and judge you! You have made us a stench to Pharaoh
and his officials and have put a sword in their
hand to kill us."

This passage reflecting Moses's first attempt at concessions from Pharaoh was by all accounts a dismal failure. Life for the Israelites was made harder, not easier, and they were punished. This can also happen with your goals as you make an attempt at improving your life and then only find that you've actually stepped backward. While this can be disheartening, it is actually helping you to discover what doesn't work.

Aaron's Staff Becomes a Snake

8 The LORD said to Moses and Aaron, 9 "When
Pharaoh says to you, 'Perform a miracle,' then say
to Aaron, 'Take your staff and throw it down before
Pharaoh,' and it will become a snake."

10 So Moses and Aaron went to Pharaoh and did just as
the LORD commanded. Aaron threw his staff down in
front of Pharaoh and his officials, and it became a snake.
11 Pharaoh then summoned wise men and sorcerers,
and the Egyptian magicians also did the same things by

their secret arts: 12 Each one threw down his staff and
it became a snake. But Aaron's staff swallowed up their
staffs. 13 Yet Pharaoh's heart became hard and he would
not listen to them, just as the LORD had said.

The example in this passage shows that Moses is working on Pharaoh's mind. Just as in your life, not everyone will support you, but that does not mean you stop planting seeds. Moses is planting the seeds to convince Pharaoh that the Lord is superior to his gods and to be feared. As you plant the seeds of change in your own life, don't expect that everyone will jump on board. You will encounter obstacles, but as Moses shows, persistence pays off.

The Plague of Blood

14 Then the LORD said to Moses, "Pharaoh's heart
is unyielding; he refuses to let the people go. 15 Go to
Pharaoh in the morning as he goes out to the water. Wait
on the bank of the Nile to meet him, and take in your
hand the staff that was changed into a snake. 16 Then
say to him, 'The LORD, the God of the Hebrews, has
sent me to say to you: Let my people go, so that they may
worship me in the desert. But until now you have not
listened. 17 This is what the LORD says: 'By this you
will know that I am the LORD: With the staff that is in
my hand I will strike the water of the Nile, and it will
be changed into blood. 18 The fish in the Nile will die,
and the river will stink; the Egyptians will not be able to
drink its water.'"

19 The LORD said to Moses, "Tell Aaron, 'Take your
staff and stretch out your hand over the waters of

Egypt—over the streams and canals, over the ponds and all the reservoirs—and they will turn to blood. Blood will be everywhere in Egypt, even in the wooden buckets and stone jars."

20 Moses and Aaron did just as the LORD had commanded. He raised his staff in the presence of Pharaoh and his officials and struck the water of the Nile, and all the water was changed into blood. 21 The fish in the Nile died, and the river smelled so bad that the Egyptians could not drink its water. Blood was everywhere in Egypt.

22 But the Egyptian magicians did the same things by their secret arts, and Pharaoh's heart became hard; he would not listen to Moses and Aaron, just as the LORD had said. 23 Instead, he turned and went into his palace, and did not take even this to heart. 24 And all the Egyptians dug along the Nile to get drinking water, because they could not drink the water of the river.

We all know of people who failed repeatedly before they finally succeeded in reaching their goals. As Moses follows God's direction, bringing plagues to Egypt, he does not meet with much success at first. I can tell you from my own experience that when you set a new course or direction, things often get worse before they get better, and as long as you know this truth, then you can prepare yourself to handle the trials that come.

The Plague of Frogs

25 Seven days passed after the LORD struck the Nile.

Exodus 8

1 Then the LORD said to Moses, "Go to Pharaoh and say to him, 'This is what the LORD says: Let my people go, so that they may worship me. 2 If you refuse to let them go, I will plague your whole country with frogs. 3 The Nile will teem with frogs. They will come up into your palace and your bedroom and onto your bed, into the houses of your officials and on your people, and into your ovens and kneading troughs. 4 The frogs will go up on you and your people and all your officials.'"

5 Then the LORD said to Moses, "Tell Aaron, 'Stretch out your hand with your staff over the streams and canals and ponds, and make frogs come up on the land of Egypt.'"

6 So Aaron stretched out his hand over the waters of Egypt, and the frogs came up and covered the land. 7 But the magicians did the same things by their secret arts; they also made frogs come up on the land of Egypt.

8 Pharaoh summoned Moses and Aaron and said, "Pray to the LORD to take the frogs away from me and my people, and I will let your people go to offer sacrifices to the LORD."

9 Moses said to Pharaoh, "I leave to you the honor of setting the time for me to pray for you and your officials and your people that you and your houses may be rid of the frogs, except for those that remain in the Nile."

10 "Tomorrow," Pharaoh said.
Moses replied, "It will be as you say, so that you may know there is no one like the LORD our God. 11 The

frogs will leave you and your houses, your officials and
your people; they will remain only in the Nile."

12 After Moses and Aaron left Pharaoh, Moses cried
out to the LORD about the frogs he had brought on
Pharaoh. 13 And the LORD did what Moses asked. The
frogs died in the houses, in the courtyards and in the
fields. 14 They were piled into heaps, and the land reeked
of them. 15 But when Pharaoh saw that there was relief,
he hardened his heart and would not listen to Moses and
Aaron, just as the LORD had said.

In this last passage, you can almost feel the anguish of Moses as Pharaoh is almost willing to concede, but then snatches back his word as soon as the plague is gone. There will be times when someone impedes your progress to the point it seems almost cruel. But remember to keep planting seeds. Keep sowing no matter what obstacles are presented. Moses continued to warn Pharaoh and bring plagues. These included a plague of gnats, a plague of flies, a plague on livestock—and it is interesting to note the plague on livestock only struck Egyptian livestock and not the livestock of the Israelites. God's plagues then began to attack Pharaoh and his people directly. The next plague was one of boils that appeared on all the Egyptians and their livestock.

The next plagues removed the food sources of the Egyptians through a plague of hail and a plague of locusts. By this time, many of the Egyptian officials were afraid and took whatever measures they could to protect their own crops and livestock. After the locusts, Moses brought a plague of darkness that so angered Pharaoh that he sent Moses away and insisted he never return to the presence of Pharaoh again.

The final plague was the plague of the firstborn that took the life of Pharaoh's firstborn as well as the firstborn of every Egyptian family. This final plague was key in finally softening Pharaoh's heart to allow the Israelites to gain their freedom.

This incident in biblical times is a wonderful example of how it sometimes can take a great deal of time and effort to achieve your goals. If Moses had given up and succumbed to the pressure from the Israelites that he was making their lives harder, he might never have helped gain their eventual freedom. In order to maintain your dream, you will also face tremendous obstacles, though probably much less than an immovable Pharaoh. But the same principles apply. You must keep trying, even if it feels like you move backward more than forward at times.

One caution is not to compare your results to those of someone else, as each person and each goal has its own germination period. It may take you six years where others achieve their goals in just a couple of years. We each travel our own path, and the overriding concept to understand is that as long as you are on the path, then each obstacle or hardship provides feedback that refines the goal and keeps you going.

10 Egyptian Plagues

1.	Water to Blood	6.	Boils
2.	Frogs	7.	Hail
3.	Gnats	8.	Locusts
4.	Flies	9.	Darkness
5.	Livestock Disease	10.	Death of First Born

CHAPTER 29

A TIME FOR PAUL!

> *If you fail to plan, you plan to fail.*
>
> **–Anonymous**

As you make decisions that will change the course of your life, you must create a new place for yourself within the life you formerly knew. A wonderful example of this transformation is the life of Paul the apostle. Paul was raised in Tarsus around the same time as Jesus, and it is likely was about ten years younger. At the time, he was known as Saul and was born of somewhat wealthy parents as he was able to purchase a Roman citizenship. During his youth, he attended a rabbinical school in Jerusalem and joined the sect of the Pharisees. The first time he is noted in the Bible is at the stoning of Stephen in the book of Acts, at which time he would have been in his early twenties.

Paul was in Jerusalem for a time, arresting and persecuting Christians on the part of the Sanhedrin, which was the highest judicial and ecclesiastical council of the Jewish nation. Paul set out on the road to Damascus where he experienced his conversion.

The most interesting part of this story is that Paul was the antithesis of what Jesus stood for. He was an enforcer of Jewish law and persecuted and killed those who didn't obey. He was one of the elite—a Roman citizen, educated Pharisee, and enforcer for the highest judicial body in the land. Paul's life transformation wasn't just an internal transformation of thought: it was a completely different life.

We've all heard the saying "You can't go home again." This is a reference to the idea that we are all changing and growing in one way or another and that even if you try to go back to the same place in time, it's not the same. One of the issues Paul encountered, and you may encounter in your life, is that when you accept new ideas and try to grow a new direction, the individuals that you thought supported you, loved you, and would be there, sometimes desert you or become very angry at the change. Even close friends and family may refuse to accept the new you and demand you "be realistic" and go back to the way things were before.

Paul had been in the elite circles of his world. By taking on the cause of Christianity, he was no longer accepted by his Jewish peers and hunted as an outlaw. There are many universal laws at work in the conversion of Paul, but a couple of them stand out. This first is the Law of Perpetual Transmutation of Energy. Everything changes—and this includes ideas and attitudes. Paul changed, but those who knew him didn't and wouldn't accept it. They branded him a traitor, and he was more hated than other Christians because he had once been in the elite Jewish circles.

Another of the laws at work is the Law of Relativity. Nothing is good unless it is compared to something else. Conversely, the conversion was seen completely differently by two sets of people. Over time, the Jewish nation came to hate Paul fiercely as a traitor to their faith and all they stood for. At the same time, as Paul spent years on missionary journeys spreading the word of Christ, the Christian community saw him as a great leader and apostle of Christ, eventually leading to sainthood. This was the same man seen completely differently by the two groups of people due to their own perspectives.

During the early years of Christianity, many of the disciples of Christ were against the idea of spreading the word to Gentiles, and they sought to preach to Jews only. Paul, on the other hand, truly grasped the concepts that Jesus taught and readily set out to spread the word to everyone who would listen. In the time right after his conversion, that was not the Jewish population. In fact, they would have loved nothing better than to get their hands on Paul and kill him as a traitor to the faith. This meant that Paul had to seek out another group, and this was the Gentiles.

Here he sets a great example for anyone wanting to accomplish a particular goal in his or her life. Things aren't always smooth—in fact they rarely are. It is only by being open and accepting of alternate paths that you will indeed reach your goals. Paul's goal was to spread the word—period. And he did not just spread the word to Jews, but to all of mankind. Had he not been so hunted by the Jews, he might not have journeyed as far as he did on his missionary journeys, and Christianity may have died out or had a much slower start.

One of the reasons Paul is so revered by Christians then and now is that he refused to accept credit for, or be exalted by, the new Christians in any way. He was very much a man of unity and a strong proponent of Christian principles, frequently admonishing the early Christians not to let petty differences come between them. We see this in the first letter to the believers in Corinth:

[10]I appeal to you, brothers, in the name of our Lord Jesus Christ, that all of you agree with one another so that there may be no divisions among you and that you may be perfectly united in mind and thought. [11]My brothers, some from Chloe's household have informed me that there are quarrels among you. [12]What I mean is this: One of you says, "I follow Paul"; another, "I follow Apollos"; another, "I follow Cephas"; still another, "I follow Christ."

[13]Is Christ divided? Was Paul crucified for you? Were you baptized into the name of Paul? [14]I am thankful that I did not baptize any of you except Crispus and Gaius, [15]so no one can say that you were baptized into my name. [16](Yes, I also baptized the household of Stephanas; beyond that, I don't remember if I baptized anyone else.) [17]For Christ did not send me to baptize, but to preach the gospel—not with words of human wisdom, lest the cross of Christ be emptied of its power.

–1 Corinthians 1:10–17 (New International Version)

Paul admonishes the followers not to get distracted and to keep their eye on the goal. This is practical advice for any person or group of people that are moving their lives beyond what they have previously known. It can be very easy to become distracted with small insignificant arguments that keep you from focusing on what is important. It is only through this focus that you will be successful.

May the grace of the Lord Jesus Christ, and the love of God, and the fellowship of the Holy Spirit be with you all.

–2 Corinthians 13:14 NIV

CHAPTER 30

LIFE'S MISSION

> *If one advances confidently in the direction of their goals
> and endeavors to live the life they have imagined, they
> will meet with success unexpected in common hours.*
>
> **–Henry David Thorough**

One of the greatest questions people often ask is what their life's mission is. Some know exactly what they were put on this earth to accomplish, others only discover it late in life, while still others never seem to find their true passion.

A person without a mission is like a feather, tossing about on the breeze, going wherever fate dictates. The leaf does not direct its path but just floats along at the whim of the wind. For some, this type of life might be exciting or adventurous, but for others who want their lives to have meant something, it can be less than fulfilling. A mission is something that you are passionate about—something that you would do for hours, days, and weeks on end with little rest and no financial reward. This does not mean that you don't deserve to be paid for your work, but the only way to feel truly alive is to find that thing you love to do that also supports you in a way that allows you to reach your goals.

For many, they spend their lives following, doing what they are told or what is expected. It is the path of least resistance for many but frequently leads to emptiness. A familiar aspect of the life of Paul is that he was constantly encouraging the believers and telling them to encourage one another.

Often when people find their true passion and mission, it involves helping others in some way. Paul acknowledged the power of personal humility and a focus on others rather than one's self.

Strength of character and courage of mission do not involve steamrolling over others. I've seen many people of various faiths who were afraid to follow their dreams because they thought that success meant they were a bad or immoral person. I think we were created to be successful in this life and, to use that success to help others.

Much like the instructions from a flight attendant to put your mask on and then help others, you can't help anyone if you aren't successful yourself. Paul did not say not to look after you own interests, but merely to also then look after the interest of others.

We were, and are, intended to fulfill our potential, and that can begin at any moment of our choosing. We each have our own will and choose our own path, which includes our goals for success. You must find the courage to make your own path. While success might not be instantaneous, it will never come if you never seek it. Just like the packet of seeds tossed into the drawer, if you never seek the environment for growth, you will not see results.

Setbacks and objections are hard to overcome as you seek your mission, but none are as hard as the negative talk and doubt in your own mind. In Jack Canfield's *The Success Principles*, belief in one's self is one of the fundamentals of success. The negative self-talk and doubt we experience is merely our own minds seeking the comfort of what we have known—even if it was a bad situation. How many people do you know who talk incessantly about how much they dislike their job, but when you suggest they get a new job, will give you a laundry list of reasons why it's not possible?

We are often our greatest obstacle. Even someone as secure in their belief as Paul in biblical times frequently went through bouts of feeling undeserving and less than he could have been:

> *⁹For I am the least of the apostles and do not even deserve to be called an apostle, because I persecuted the church of God. ¹⁰But by the grace of God I am what I am, and his grace to me was not without effect. No, I worked harder than all of them—yet not I, but the grace of God that was with me. ¹¹Whether, then, it was I or they, this is what we preach, and this is what you believed.*

–1 Corinthians 15:9–11 (New International Version)

Paul had every reason to doubt his worth—he had persecuted and killed the very people he now served—but he didn't allow that feeling to stop him. He knew he was on track and kept working hard—harder than all the rest by his own admission.

We all have moments of self-doubt or feelings that we are undeserving at times. The important point is to know that these feelings are fleeting if you will focus on the goal and not on yourself. One of the dangers of turning inward on yourself every time something goes wrong or not as well as you hoped is that you change the vibration you send out and therefore manifest even more negative events and actions. The Law of Attraction states that we will return to ourselves that which we dwell on. Paul knew this to be true, and even during his time in prison, when he could have been sitting in his cell feeling angry at those who imprisoned him or sorry for himself, he was instead writing letters to his follows about loving one another and sticking to the principles of Christianity. He stayed focused on the goal and did what he could through the written word to help others improve their lives. Those words have been read by people in every generation and every country in existence to this day.

You have no idea the eventual good that will come from your living a purposeful life full of joy and excitement for the day ahead. I picture Paul sitting alone in a horrible jail cell, treated like a dog and scum of the earth. He had tremendous belief in his life's mission—not because he had any idea that anyone would remember his name after he was gone (in fact he probably would have preferred they didn't), but because he was growing himself as a person and keeping the idea of Christianity afloat amid very intense and dangerous times.

Fear is a mighty foe for each of us no matter where we are in our lives. Fear can strike the most secure billionaire and the average housewife. It is no respecter of people, cultures, or religious beliefs and comes in all forms and fashions.

Some choose to use their emotion of fear to spur them on to greater heights, and this is a wonderful attitude. But I've also come across a number of people who refuse the idea that they experience fear at all. I have to wonder if they were in a tank of water and saw a fin pop up, if they'd be so sure they never experienced fear!

The reason fear is talked of so much is that it makes people do, and believe, crazy things sometimes. When Columbus set out across the Atlantic Ocean, there was real fear among the sailors that the ship would reach the edge of the earth and fall right off. This was due to their belief that the world was flat, and though it sounds ridiculous to us now, it made for many a sleepless night on that sea voyage.

¹If you have any encouragement from being united with Christ, if any comfort from his love, if any fellowship with the Spirit, if any tenderness and compassion, ²then make my joy complete by being like-minded, having the same love, being one in spirit and purpose. ³Do nothing out of selfish ambition or vain conceit, but in humility consider others better than yourselves. ⁴Each of you should look not only to your own interests, but also to the interests of others.

–Philippians 2:1–5 (New International Version)

CHAPTER 31

FALSE EVIDENCE APPEARING REAL

> *Genius is 1 percent inspiration and 99 percent perspiration*
>
> **–Thomas Edison**

When David took up his slingshot to face the mighty Goliath, he was afraid—no doubt about it. Yet he used that fear to his advantage. It would have been easy for him to run, and one of the reasons this story is so inspiring is that he chose to face that fear and believe that he would be victorious.

Fear can also make us do strange things in the name of faith, and we see this going back to the example of the Essenes. They sequestered themselves away from the world, claiming they couldn't be with other nonbelievers, as it would contaminate them. We see this today with factions of religious groups that have a leader who is all-powerful and insists that the followers separate themselves from family and friends and live only with other believers. Fear allows leaders of these people to maintain an iron grip on the minds of the followers, and they then use fear to keep the outside world from interfering. This reminds me of the Essenes.

Not only were these types of thought processes pushed aside by Christ himself, but the very nature of faith and universal laws hinges on the underlying knowledge that we are all connected no matter how hard we may try to separate ourselves. We are not separate, so to try and create groups, divisions, or factions among various peoples is a detriment to us all in the long run.

One of the longest held divides in the history of humanity is that between religion and science. As evidenced through this book, and the work of many other philosophers, thinkers, and authors, science and religion are not only connected, but strongly connected. There are no two schools of thought as many would have you believe. Both sides seek the same answers, and both sides come to the same conclusions, though they call them different names. Science may call it laws of the universe; religion may call it teachings of Christ, or the Torah, or the I Ching, or any of a number of texts. The bottom line is that they resemble one another far more than they diverge from one another in respect to how we are to treat others and how we are to have courage and faith.

As you travel your chosen path, the people you choose to share that path with can and will have a tremendous effect on you, as you will on them.

In churches around the world, the faithful are admonished to gather together and support one another. This is a good thing, as we are mentally encouraged by being around those who are like-minded.

I also see many who have embraced the ideas presented in *The Secret* who are associating together with great teachers and leaders to achieve similar goals and ideals based on understanding the laws of the universe and how they work with religious faith rather than against it. It is interesting, but some of the most vocal opponents of these "new" ideas are religious leaders. The universal laws basically state everything you ever learned in Sunday school, which include:

- Everything changes, and you can change for the better.

- What you think makes a difference in how you see things.

- You gravitate toward people like yourself and toward events you have in common.

- For every yes there is a no.

- The seasons cycle endlessly according to God's plan.

- There are rewards and/or consequences for every thought or action.

- Things come about in God's time, not your own.

These principles appear in every religious text in the world in some way. This is because they are universal truths, not personal growth, or American, or any other kind of truth. They apply to all people everywhere.

Fear can keep those of religious faith from embracing these ideas because they may feel their particular religion to be threatened by embracing something new, but that does not have to be the case. Knowing and embracing these truths doesn't mean you have to partake of everything, nor does it mean you have to shut yourself off from the world. It merely gives you the slingshot—you still must have faith and belief that you will be victorious. We are a planet of imperfect beings striving for more in our lives, and we will make mistakes, but that's okay. That's how it was intended for us to learn. As we travel our paths and expand our understanding, we are not leaving anything behind, including our faith. We are bringing it along and adding more knowledge and power that will help us create the life we want.

²¹*From that time on Jesus began to explain to his disciples that he must go to Jerusalem and suffer many things at the hands of the elders, chief priests and teachers of the law, and that he must be killed and on the third day be raised to life.* ²²*Peter took him aside and began to rebuke him. "Never, Lord!" he said. "This shall never happen to you!"* ²³*Jesus turned and said to Peter, "Get behind me, Satan! You are a stumbling block to me; you do not have in mind the things of God, but the things of men."* ²⁴*Then Jesus said to his disciples, "If anyone would come after me, he must deny himself and take up his cross and follow me.* ²⁵*For whoever wants to save his life will lose it, but whoever loses his life for me will find it.* ²⁶*What good will it be for a man if he gains the whole world, yet forfeits his soul? Or what can a man give in exchange for his soul?*

–Matthew 16:21–26 (New International Version)

CHAPTER 32

THE POWER OF THE SUBCONSCIOUS MIND

> *As a man thinketh in his heart, so is he*
>
> **–The Bible**

Our minds are made up of two distinct areas that work together to allow us to perceive our world. These are the conscious and subconscious mind. According to Bob Proctor, the conscious mind is 5 percent of the brain, and the subconscious is 95 percent. We know that many of the body's functions, such as breathing, happen on a nonconscious level, and we have little to no power of control over these bodily functions that keep us alive. We do have a great deal of control over our conscious minds and less control of our subconscious minds.

The conscious mind is our awareness. When we are awake, we are taking in everything that occurs in the world around us. This information is filtered through our RAS (reticular activating system), which is the area of the brain in charge of how we perceive the world and how we respond to stimuli that is beyond reflex. Judgments, decisions, and logical thought are created and put into action by the RAS. Dreams, visions, and even hallucinations, are created by the RAS as it responds to under- or overstimulation.

We each have literally thousands of thoughts each day, and the RAS has to have a filtering system to prioritize them or we would be so bombarded by stimuli, we could never get anything done. This filtering system is created in a very specific way.

Throughout our lives, as we learn and are taught various ideas, they act as our first filters. They say x is more important than y, and y is more important than c, and so on. An example might be food is more important than pleasure, and pleasure is more important than pain. As we grow and experience life, these ideas become ingrained in the subconscious mind as beliefs, or paradigms, and are very specific. These may include positive ideas such as, "I can become highly educated," or "I deserve to be well treated," or even "I am successful in every area." Unfortunately, they may also include negative ideas such as, "I will never be a healthy weight," "No one cares about me," or "I'm not successful no matter how hard I try."

Every person has a mixed bag of beliefs and ideas created by what we learn from others and from our experiences as we age. These are stored in the subconscious and used to filter every experience from that point forward. While this system usually works well, it also has some drawbacks that can work against you if you are unaware of them. If you are convinced that you are not successful, then you are telling your subconscious to ignore all of the opportunities for success that present themselves each day.

While this may sound ridiculous, it is true and working each day. A good example is if you go to a car lot and see a new shiny bright blue car. You think that it is unique, but the minute you drive it off the lot, you suddenly see every bright blue car on the highway! It's not that they weren't there before—they were. But your mind filtered them out as unimportant. The same thing happens in every area of life, depending on the beliefs and ideas that you hold in your subconscious.

Another example is if you believe that you will never find your soulmate. Your mind then understands that this person does not exist and therefore doesn't look for him or her. That is why this type of belief is self-fulfilling—as you tell your mind what you believe to be so, it accepts those thoughts as fact. So even if you meet wonderful people every day that you might start a relationship with, your mind will prevent you from seeing the possibilities.

Our subconscious minds are often so clogged with old beliefs and paradigms that we wonder who we really are without all these other ideas we have floating around in our heads. While you can go back to childhood and discover the real you, you can choose to quiet the noise in your brain for a specified amount of time to clarify what you really want and what you really believe. One exercise to trigger this is to engage in what is known as stream of consciousness, or right-brained, writing.

I'm sure you've heard the arguments for right-brained and left-brained. This refers to the idea that certain functions of the mind are relegated to particular areas of the brain. Predominately, the left hemisphere of the brain contains more analytical skills, such as math, language, and problem solving, while the right hemisphere of the brain contains more abstract ideas, such as the creative, intuitive, and spiritual functions.

What many don't realize is that both sides of your brain work together at all times, but not always in balance. If you are a novelist writing a book, then you need creativity, but you also need language skills, so the hemispheres need to have similar levels of activity, and if you were an accountant looking for deductions for a client, you would use the logic and math centers on the left side of the brain and the intuition and creativity on the right.

When the brain function is out of balance, we know it and can feel it. We often refer to these moments as mind numbing, which can happen if you are focused on one intense and selective activity for a time. Data entry is a good example. It is repetitive and lacks any need for creativity or intuition or anything that the right side of the brain can provide. It does not challenge the brain, and it literally feels like half of your brain has fallen asleep—which it hasn't—but it does show a marked decrease in blood flow and activity.

As your brain developed when you were a child, it *lateralized* functions. In other words, it placed the control centers for some functions on the right side and the control centers for others on the left, relegating them to particular areas. Most of our brains are organized in a similar fashion, so we know in general terms where each person's language center will be or each person's intuitive center.

With this knowledge, we can choose to increase activity in a given portion of the brain by focusing on certain activities or ideas. In order to uncover your true wants and desires without all the clutter of old beliefs and paradigms, you can engage in right-brained writing. This means letting words flow from your pen without editing or prompting—basically without conscious thought. You might write a memory from childhood, a paragraph about your pet, or even how much you dislike cell phones— whatever is on your mind at the moment. This is intended to give you insight into who you are and what you really think.

Rarely do we say or write down what we really think. Most of our thoughts are put through the filters we have created over time, and we edit them accordingly, often to the point that we don't ever verbalize what we want or don't want. By doing this type of writing for five minutes every day, over time, it will become clear what you really want and what your true innate talents are—as long as you don't allow your internal critic to switch on while you write. Often people will do some of this type of writing, and when they read it over, they disagree with everything on the page. This is the fear we discussed earlier. If you write about cooking and how much you love it and relive the old dream you once had to own a restaurant, you shouldn't let that "logical" part of your brain convince you that its folly. Often that logic is your own paradigms speaking in fear rather than supporting your own heart's desires.

I read about a lawyer who, when he was in college, was a local surfer who was well-known and liked by everyone on the beach. He would sit and talk for hours about how he wanted to someday own a fish taco stand near the beach so that he could surf as much as he wanted and enjoy life. But his father was a lawyer, and his father before him. My friend followed the expected path, endured law school, and joined the family law firm and hated it. He felt trapped. He spent all this time and money to become a lawyer, and the idea of tossing that away was something he couldn't justify.

After practicing for over ten years at the law firm, this friend had a reunion with some of his old college buddies—none of whom could believe he was in a shirt and tie all day. When my friend started to once again talk about his dream of owning a fish taco stand near the beach, his buddy stopped him and asked, "When do think you're going to get this 'someday?' Life isn't a trial run, and you don't get a second chance just because you wasted the first one pleasing everyone else."

Within a month, he had quit the firm, and even though his family thought he'd had a nervous breakdown, he opened his first taco stand. Now he has an entire chain of more than 25 small beachfront restaurants near the best surfing locations in the world. One might argue that his education and experience was wasted, but was it? I don't think so. After ten years practicing law, he had enough knowledge to run a business successfully and grow it into a franchise. He was aware of the pitfalls and what to avoid. Had he started the business right out of school, he would not have had that same level of knowledge.

It may be hard to get past the ideas holding you into the life you now live. It feels like you are stuck and have no choice, but you do. There is no rule that says your life must follow a certain pattern of events; you create that pattern each day. You have the power to insert new beliefs and ideas into your subconscious mind that are positive and allow you to see the possibilities. This is why so many gurus say that, to succeed, you must take that first step, and the path will become clear. The reason is that until you overcome your fear and old beliefs, your subconscious will not allow you to see the way. But once you focus on what you want and take that first step, you reorder the mind to a different set of filters and priorities. The veil of darkness lifts, and you see all the help you need was right in front of you the whole time, just like the blue cars on the highway.

³For what the law was powerless to do in that it was weakened by the sinful nature, God did by sending his own Son in the likeness of sinful man to be a sin offering. And so he condemned sin in sinful man, ⁴in order that the righteous requirements of the law might be fully met in us, who do not live according to the sinful nature but according to the Spirit. ⁵Those who live according to the sinful nature have their minds set on what that nature desires; but those who live in accordance with the Spirit have their minds set on what the Spirit desires. ⁶The mind of sinful man is death, but the mind controlled by the Spirit is life and peace; ⁷the sinful mind is hostile to God. It does not submit to God's law, nor can it do so. ⁸Those controlled by the sinful nature cannot please God.

–Romans 8:3–8 (New International Version)

CHAPTER 33

BUT I WANT IT *NOW!*

Great works are performed not by strength,
but by perseverance

–Samuel Johnson

We live in a fast-paced world where instantaneous gratification is the norm. Want a book? Click to order. Want to read it now? Download online. Want a roast beef dinner or lasagna? Five minutes from freezer to plate in the microwave. Too hungry to wait a whole five minutes? Two minutes to reheat last night's leftovers. We have come to expect that we can talk to anyone anywhere in the world instantly, and for the most part, we can. Now contrast that with the idea of the Law of Gestation and Gender that states that every idea has a gestation period or incubation period, and you can see that there could be a problem for many people these days. We want what we want, and we want it *now!*

Ideas are spiritual seeds and will move into form or physical results when the time is right and the environment to grow the idea comes into being. Your goals will manifest—know that they will and have faith. I realize that may not help much when you are striving toward your goal when it seems as far away as ever. It can be tempting to allow negative feelings to enter into your mind when others seem to achieve the same goal so easily.

Your subconscious mind takes time to reorder itself, and you must continually focus on your goal in order to achieve what you really want. For many people, the ideas and beliefs that they have held all their lives can crowd back in and get them off track once again. It is like trying to follow a blinking light in the darkness—you must focus and wait for the next step or direction.

It is during these times that it is of the utmost importance to send good wishes to those who are achieving those things that you want to achieve. To not do so allows jealousy and anger to manifest rather than the positive realization of your goals. This was especially a problem with the early Christians who had been used to the idea of "an eye for an eye" and were very prone to jealousy and ill will toward others.

> [12] *Now we ask you, brothers, to respect those who work*
> *hard among you, who are over you in the Lord and*
> *who admonish you.* [13] *Hold them in the highest regard*
> *in love because of their work. Live in peace with each*
> *other.* [14] *And we urge you, brothers, warn those who are*

idle, encourage the timid, help the weak, be patient with everyone. [15] Make sure that nobody pays back wrong for wrong, but always try to be kind to each other and to everyone else.

[16] Be joyful always; [17] pray continually; [18] give thanks in all circumstances, for this is God's will for you in Christ Jesus.

[19] Do not put out the Spirit's fire; [20] do not treat prophecies with contempt. [21] Test everything. Hold on to the good. [22] Avoid every kind of evil.

–I Thessalonians 5:12–22

There is a reason that patience is a virtue. It is due to the fact that it is so hard for us to exhibit in all areas of our life. For most people these days, it is exacerbated by the fact that we are constantly pulled in so many directions. When we are multitasking or on a tight timeline, we tend to be short-tempered and impatient. We have to-do lists that are way too long and unrealistic for the given timeframe. Even if you feel that there's no help for the list, there usually is, and that includes delegating some of the items and eliminating others that aren't really important. The lack of patience is linked to simply feeling overwhelmed, and when you are overwhelmed, your emotions flare.

Each person has his or her own personal triggers, and by becoming aware of these triggers, you will increase your patience and lower your stress level. If you feel anxious or worried, it heightens your sensitivity to these triggers. It could be an event (dinner with the family), a person (your ex), or even just a phrase ("You're just like your mother") that can push our buttons and lead you to overreact. This is the point where people will have the tendency to give up on their goal. Rather than understanding that it takes time, they feel overwhelmed and angry and just want to give up rather than continue to do those things that will eventually lead them to success.

You can picture in your mind that you plant a seed in a pot outside. It has access to sun, water, and clean air. But if every time you see storm clouds, you bring the pot inside, the plant will never weather a storm to get the life-giving water it needs. This is important because the storms you weather on the way to achieving your goals make you stronger and bring about the environment to help manifest those goals.

Developing patience requires a change in attitude and understanding yourself. Once you understand what triggers your impatience, you can take steps to recognize the early stages of impatience and start using some relaxation techniques or remove yourself from the situation. In an earlier chapter, we talked about guarding your conscious mind and how allowing repeated bouts of impatience to manifest is damaging to your positive mental attitude.

Even in biblical times, when life was much slower, people struggled with patience, and we still do. We are still the same, although life has changed dramatically in the ensuing centuries. Pursuing your dreams is very much about reminding yourself that things take time. Rushing into a plan full force without allowing it to incubate invites failure and frustration. Some would say that incubating an idea is just an excuse to waste time, and when gratification isn't quickly forthcoming, we quickly conclude it's not working and try something else.

I'm sure you know someone who is constantly trying something new—yet never seems to finish anything. I have a friend who is constantly sharing her "little brother" stories. Though well past middle age, her brother is constantly coming up with one scheme after another that will make him rich. Over the years, he's tried his hand at being a medical tech, owning a paint and dent repair shop, selling premium knives, selling pots and pans, starting a restaurant, running a landscape business, owning a fencing business, and most recently, being a professional poker player! It's not that any of these goals or ideals were wrong, but he never gave any of them the time to germinate and grow. When things got hard, he just gave up.

Even if you've seen this pattern in your own life, that doesn't mean you can't change or that this time you will fail. You must understand that you must forgive yourself and allow your mind to dream. Many people fail repeatedly at various endeavors and eventually become convinced that they are failures. This is not true. We create our futures by what we do today, not what we have or haven't done in the past. Each day starts anew and allows us the privilege of creating our world all over again and trying something new.

When trying to change your life, the most important things you can focus on are those that matter. Doing inconsequential activities creates frustration and impatience. As you move toward being kind, generous, and supportive of others, your gratitude will attract those things you need to succeed. Take time to remember that focusing on others reduces your tendency to want something different right now and allows your ideas to come to full fruition.

> ²³*Yet a time is coming and has now come when the true worshipers will worship the Father in spirit and truth, for they are the kind of worshipers the Father seeks.* ²⁴*God is spirit, and his worshipers must worship in spirit and in truth.*
>
> **–John 4:23–24 (New International Version)**

[12]Now we ask you, brothers, to respect those who work hard among you, who are over you in the Lord and who admonish you. [13]Hold them in the highest regard in love because of their work. Live in peace with each other. [14]And we urge you, brothers, warn those who are idle, encourage the timid, help the weak, be patient with everyone. [15]Make sure that nobody pays back wrong for wrong, but always try to be kind to each other and to everyone else. [16]Be joyful always; [17]pray continually; [18]give thanks in all circumstances, for this is God's will for you in Christ Jesus. [19]Do not put out the Spirit's fire; [20]do not treat prophecies with contempt. [21]Test everything. Hold on to the good. [22]Avoid every kind of evil.

–1 Thessalonians 5:12–22 (New International Version)

CHAPTER 34

HELP! I'VE FALLEN, AND I AM AFRAID

Man's mind, once stretched by a new idea, never regains its original dimensions.

–Oliver Wendell Holmes

So let's say that you set out toward your goal and have been trying valiantly to make a go of it, but alas, you fail. It feels as if you can't do anything right, and all your past failures play in your mind like a cruel movie as if to highlight how little hope you really have. Why is this? It's as if someone has drained all the hope and belief from your body and replaced it with absolute fear.

While it may seem like the pit of despair, this response is actually quite normal due to the way our brains work. Dr. Maxwell Maltz wrote a book on the subject entitled *Psycho-Cybernetics* almost 50 years ago that explains that we each have a built-in set point for success in various areas of our lives. This creates our comfort zones, which include finances, relationships, and achievements, as well as many other areas. We perceive ourselves to "fit" into a certain life and lifestyle, and when we try to push beyond what we are used to, we become very uncomfortable and will experience frequent setbacks.

This idea explains why some people struggle to kick certain habits, or lose weight, or to be financially successful. Each time they try, their old beliefs and ideas fight to keep them where they are. In order to create a new set point for a particular area of life, it requires long-term focused concentration—but it can be done. It is just important to understand that it is a process, and one try at something will not make you successful. It takes many attempts, and some failure, to move forward. We must start at the beginning of the learning process and learn all over again as we did when we were children.

We learn in a particular way that consists of four stages. As we are children, we go about our days blissfully unaware that we are unable to do certain things. This stage is called *unconscious incompetence*. Often when we are in a new situation, we may not be aware of what we are doing wrong—in other words, we don't know what we don't know. This is much like a child who does not know how to ride a bicycle. The child would not see a need for transportation or even know what a bicycle was for. The child does not see the need for knowledge because he isn't aware of a problem. The same is true in our own live. We may not see the need for personal growth because we are floating along through life as we always have and don't realize there's something better for us.

At some point, either through another person or from our own realization, we come to the knowledge that we don't know something, whether it is a task, behavior, or idea. Those at this stage admit to themselves and possibly to others that there is something they don't know. This is the awareness stage that so many people speak about. It is not until we acknowledge that we can't do something that we can acknowledge and understand we need help. The child sees another child on a bicycle and wants to ride, too. A person with many failed relationships recognizes he or she has to learn new skills to be successful in a new relationship.

Once the awareness is raised, the person moves on to the next stage known as *conscious competence*, where you know how to do something, but you must focus and concentrate to complete the task. This is the most difficult stage. You can do the task or grasp the idea, but you don't have it down perfectly. It takes a tremendous amount of focus and concentration for you to perform, and it takes longer for you than for others who already are familiar. The child can ride the bicycle but wobbles, falls off, and has many starts and stops. The person trying to achieve personal growth does so in spurts, and only when he or she is actively thinking about it—other times they fall into old habits. This third stage is when many people may quit. Learning something new takes effort and concentration, and you are bound to make mistakes, but it is only by performing the task or behavior repeatedly that you will truly learn.

The last stage of learning is *unconscious competence*, which means that you now can perform the task almost without thinking about it. It has become part of your subconscious to the point that even if you leave the task and come back to it years later, you can still perform it well. Just as the child who learned to ride a bicycle. Even after decades of not being on a bicycle, the adult can hop on and immediately begin to ride. The person who learns new tools for successful relationships can find someone to be with long term.

It is only by performing a particular skill repeatedly that the brain creates additional neural pathways that allow us to perform the skill without conscious thought and to ingrain this as a belief. As we go through our lives, learning and growing, these skills are enhanced and added on to, and we become able to do more and process more information.

There is a concept called *brain plasticity*. This idea is that when you learn a new skill, you create a connection between two areas in your brain. When you reinforce this new information through repetition, you reinforce the cellular structure or the cellular cluster in your brain to the point that you go from conscious competence to unconscious competence.

We encounter billions of bits of information as we go through our lives, which is all useless information unless our brains can make sense of it. By conditioning your brain on what to do with the information, you sort through what is relevant and what is not in an instant, gaining information and behaviors that will help you to achieve your goals.

The idea of fear may seem to have many components, but in reality, it is the brain being challenged by an unknown. This unknown may be if your new business will grow, or if that relationship will survive—or even if that fin in the water will result in being bitten in half! Think back to when you were a child. What did you fear? The dark? The monster in the closet? The dust bunnies under the bed? Losing your parents' love? All of these have one thing in common—the unknown. Fear may seem to come in different forms, but it can inevitably be boiled down to this one truth.

I often marvel at people who are what I consider extreme risk takers— those that bungee jump from bridges, play the commodity market, or are professional gamblers. How can these people endure so much risk in their daily lives? To me, it would be frightening to live with everything I had, including my very life, at risk all the time. However, for these people, they have experience in this level of risk. They have worked at learning their skill and no longer see it as a risk. This is the Law of Relativity at work again. Once we become unconsciously competent in an area, our brain takes it off the high-risk list, and we don't even think about it being risky anymore.

I speak in front of people all the time and have absolutely no fear of doing so. I've talked in front of dignitaries and CEOs, housewives and millionaires, and think nothing of stepping on a stage no matter who is in the audience. Yet I know many people who would never do so. They are so fearful of speaking to a group, they literally make themselves sick to the point of having heart palpitations. For me, it is amazing they could have such fear of something I don't even think twice about, but again, all is relative. I have a comfort level because I have become unconsciously competent, and it is no longer an unknown for me. They are afraid because it is a great unknown to them.

When we forge forward, we will occasionally feel fearful, and that's perfectly natural. But we must move past that fear and concentrate on learning the skills necessary to remove the fear and keep it from impeding our progress.

Trials and Temptations

[2]*Consider it pure joy, my brothers, whenever you face trials of many kinds,* [3]*because you know that the testing of your faith develops perseverance.* [4]*Perseverance must finish its work so that you may be mature and complete, not lacking anything.* [5]*If any of you lacks wisdom, he should ask God, who gives generously to all without finding fault, and it will be given to him.* [6]*But when he asks, he must believe and not doubt, because he who doubts is like a wave of the sea, blown and tossed by the wind.* [7]*That man should not think he will receive anything from the Lord;* [8]*he is a double-minded man, unstable in all he does.*

–James 1:2–8 (New International Version)

CHAPTER 35

ACTS/GOALS

> *The pessimist sees the difficulty in every opportunity. An optimist sees the opportunity in every difficulty.*
>
> **–Sir Winston Churchill**

The last chapter in Acts states that the Holy Spirit sure knew what he was talking about when he addressed the ancient people through Isaiah the prophet: "Go to these people and tell them this, you are going to listen with your ears but you won't hear a word. You are going to see with your eyes but you won't see a thing." The Jews were apparently a little hardheaded. They'd even physically stick their fingers in their ears so that they would not have to listen. The screwed their eyes shut so that they did not have to look or deal face to face with their issues and let God heal them. "You've had your chance," is what the Holy Spirit implied through Isaiah. The non-Jewish outsiders, on the otherhand, were ready to receive the new ideas of Christianity with open arms.

I've encountered many patients who reacted in a similar fashion when dealing with their paradigms and beliefs about their health. Paradigms are limiting beliefs about one's self that prevent someone from moving forward in life, whether physically, mentally, spiritually, emotionally, or financial. Physicians should encourage their patients and help them recognize the fact that their beliefs are not serving them well and in many instances are keeping them ill. It is common for someone's negative outlook on life and focus on illness to keep that person from healing. While many doctors may be tempted to suggest another pill, it is probably not the underlying cause of the issue.

I have a patient, we'll call her Ida, who sees me on a regular basis. When you talk to Ida, you hear all about her kids and grandkids as well as the antics of her Chihuahua, Lucy. Ida has had some medical concerns in the past, but they are being managed well and have been for several years. Still, about once a month, she comes to see me for some small or insignificant complaint. Does she need medical care? Not really. Does she need someone to talk to? Absolutely. I've discussed the idea of her getting out and participating at her church more or at the local senior center many times, but each and every time I suggest something, she says, "Well that's for those old folks, not for me." By refusing to accept the coming of age, Ida instead isolates herself and is actually aging much faster than other women her age who have active social lives. Ida's paradigm of refusing to accept her age is actually attracting age at a faster rate.

We all have various beliefs and paradigms about everything from love to career to finances, and to religion. Many of these beliefs we have because we were raised with them, while others have been developed through our personal life experience. These beliefs can hold us back, and the paradigms buried in our unconscious mind prevent us from living the purpose God intended us for.

Each occupation or role we play in the family structure has its own areas that are affected by our past beliefs. Ministers and priests have paradigms built through their religious training and easily block ideas that don't fit into that "known" box. We also have paradigms about finances and what kind of career we might have. You may love to sing but have been convinced growing up that you aren't good enough to do well and that you can't make a living at it anyway. Parents often unconsciously plant these ideas in our heads when they make comments, and children absorb them. Have you ever heard someone say they were self-employed, and you immediately thought "unemployed"? That is a paradigm popping up in your brain. Have you ever seen someone flaunting his money and labeled him in your mind "overleveraged"? What about if your children are in college and one calls home saying she wants to be an English major? Would your first reaction be, "Why, you can't make any money at that!" We keep ourselves stuck in endless cycles of emotional and financial stress, worry, and panic, all from these paradigms that may not really even apply to our lives anymore.

The unconscious mind does what it is told to do. It does not make judgments as to right or wrong, but rather accepts the information and instructions given. It repeats what it has learned from others, habits it has been taught, and the attitudes picked up from family and friends.

The first six years of our lives we absorb everything we are told. Our minds are like sponges, taking it all in as fact, though we don't really have the ability to discern fact from fiction at this age. This is why most children learn that there is no Santa Clause around age five or six (unless someone tells them earlier) because at this point they are beginning to discern information and reason through it on their own. Young children have an amazing capacity for language and can learn however many languages they are exposed to during that period of time. This ability diminishes over time, but if learned early, it stays with them the rest of their lives.

When we are young, we learn good habits and bad habits, many of which can serve us quite well. However, we also establish habits that do not serve us well and which may prevent us from achieving our goals. As we mature, they can prevent us from achieving God's purpose in our lives unless we realize the problem or it is pointed out to us (unconscious incompetence).

It is well-known that stories play an integral part in our ability to learn. This is due to the fact that stories allow us to create visual images in our mind and therefore use more portions of the brain. This increases our memory due to the increased number of neuron connections.

There is a story that Joe Vitale frequently tells that highlights the limitations of our beliefs. Joe once had a dog named Spot, a stray that he claimed as his own when he was in college. The dog would run through and tear up the neighbor's garden, run across the road and make drivers slam on their brakes, and just make a general nuisance of himself. So Joe put a leash on him but felt guilty for keeping this wonderful friend on a three-foot leash. He bought a longer leash and gave him six feet of freedom. Joe then walked six feet away and called Spot. He ran three feet. The dog wouldn't go an inch beyond the length of the old leash because he knew the leash had always been three feet and had no idea this new leash gave him more freedom. Joe walked over to Spot and encouraged him to walk out the full six feet of the new leash. He planted a new belief in Spot's mind, and from then on, the dog used all six feet of the leash. Spot had a new paradigm, a new belief about the leash. While this is a simple story, it illustrates an important idea in that we often limit ourselves without even realizing it.

I knew a couple a few years ago whose daughter was attending a prestigious university. While in school, the daughter worked as an administrative assistant. When she graduated, the daughter sent out resumes—but only for jobs as an administrative assistant that offered virtually the same pay level she'd been receiving. Without realizing it, she had created a paradigm in her own mind that she was an administrative assistant and that was what she was meant to be. Once this was pointed out, she was shocked and amazed that she'd so limited herself. She opened her mind and decided to add a nursing certificate to her degree and is now a nursing supervisor at a local hospital. Had this never been pointed out to her early on she might still be an overqualified, overeducated administrative assistant!

It is important to understand that we all create limits in our minds that we must continually guard against. There is a story about a scientist who was studying fleas. He placed a number of fleas in a glass jar, and the jar was four inches high (like a baby food jar). The fleas would jump and hit their heads on the top of the jar. They did this for a day, and at the end of the day, the top was removed from the jar. When the top was removed, the fleas jumped to where they had been hitting the top and would not jump any further. They had established their limit. When they were taken out of the jar and moved back in the open world, they continued to only jump the two inches rather than the eight or ten inches they were able to jump to as fleas. They were born with that capability, like the dog, to move from one animal to another animal or one place within an animal to another. When they were trapped, they moved to a new paradigm.

Jesus recognized the limiting beliefs that people carried. He regularly told the disciples they could do anything they had witnessed or chose to do, it only required faith that the old habits could be changed and they could grow and fulfill God's purpose for their lives. But it required a change or shift in beliefs.

John Assaraf tells the story about a fellow that was driving a beautiful convertible on a delightful day in California. He was driving through the countryside, enjoying the ride. As he began to turn to the right, he noticed another convertible right in front of him that was coming toward him. A beautiful blonde was driving that car. As she passed him, she shouted out, "Pig, pig!" That immediately changed his opinion and altered his perspective to think that the girl was no longer the beauty he had assumed her to be. As the man turned at the curve in the road, he saw to his surprise that there was a pig in the middle of the road. The woman was trying to warn him, yet he had created an erroneous belief of what she was like from her actions.

How many times have you done the same and established a belief without appropriate study, and then something happened to change your mind? I know a man who was a lay preacher for many years and very conservative in his beliefs. Though he was a good man, he was convinced that homosexuals were evil and refused to have anything to do with them. When his wife retired, they moved to Santa Fe to be near their daughter, and this man got a job working in the local hospital emergency room. There were many gay and lesbian individuals who worked in the hospital. After working with them for a few months, he realized his point of view had been incorrect. He could do more good through love for his fellow workers than through judgment and condemnation. While many of us talk about God being the final judge, we are still prone to make judgments that can inhibit our spiritual growth.

In many ways, he depends on us to find the path. We must have faith in God and accept the purpose we feel directed to in order to achieve the intention that we were created for.

> [7]Be patient, then, brothers, until the Lord's coming. See how the farmer waits for the land to yield its valuable crop and how patient he is for the autumn and spring rains. [8]You too, be patient and stand firm, because the Lord's coming is near.
>
> –James 5:7–8 (New International Version)

CHAPTER 36

GIVING IN GRATITUDE

> *You cannot teach a man anything, you can only help him find it within himself*
>
> **–Galileo Galilei**

Gratitude is one of the most wonderful emotions one can experience. Not only does it uplift you, it uplifts others that you are thankful for. Gratitude helps you focus on those items and people in your life that are positive and helping you achieve your goals. As you focus on them through gratitude each day, the more positive events come to you through the Law of Attraction. Gratitude is extremely powerful, and I recommend that individuals keep a gratitude journal, writing each day those things they are most grateful for. The idea of gratitude and giving go hand in hand and have a multitude of meanings for those inside and outside of traditional religious settings.

> *⁷Each man should give what he has decided in his heart to give, not reluctantly or under compulsion, for God loves a cheerful giver.*

> **–2 Corinthians 9:7 (New International Version)**

Anyone who has spent more than a few hours in a traditional religious organization has been asked to give. Oftentimes we think this is in reference to monetary giving, and it is, but that is only one small portion. It is also in reference to giving of yourself, your time, your knowledge, and your skill to others. Jesus even pointed this out when the Pharisees tried to trap him into saying that Jews and Christians shouldn't pay taxes to Rome:

> *¹⁸ But Jesus, knowing their evil intent, said, "You hypocrites, why are you trying to trap me?*

> *¹⁹ Show me the coin used for paying the tax." They brought him a denarius,*

> *²⁰ and he asked them, "Whose portrait is this? And whose inscription?"*

> *²¹ "Caesar's," they replied.*
> *Then he said to them, "Give to Caesar what is Caesar's, and to God what is God's."*

> **–Matthew 22:10–21**

Giving isn't about monetary assets that support a church. It is about giving of yourself with those things, talent, time, and knowledge, as well as financial assets that God has given you and to do so with a grateful heart. Now, I've known many people of many faiths, and I've seen personally that, yes, there is such a thing as an uncheerful giver! In fact, I'd call them begrudging givers. They constantly complain about the little details of money they think the church is wasting or what they would do with it instead. This is not God's intention for the focus of our giving.

We do not give to receive, but receive we will if we are in a state of gratitude. One of the areas that people will often comment on is that they think if they give God $100, that God will return them $1,000—but this is not the case. God will return to you in larger measure, but it may not be in cash. That which you give to may not be the instrument that God chooses to bless you through, so the expectation of gaining from God because you wrote a check to the church means that you have nullified the intention of giving. If you only give to gain, you will not gain. But if you give out of the sheer joy of giving and in absolute gratitude, you will gain.

I knew a woman from a small town that had a Methodist church and a Baptist church. She shared that the two churches sat on corners of subsequent blocks on one of the main streets in town. Though everyone knew everyone in town, there was a clear divide with who socialized with whom based on church affiliation. There was also often an undercurrent of rivalry between the congregations over the years.

Late one winter night, as a light snow fell, a small fire due to an electrical short flickered and took hold in the Methodist church, which burned to the ground. The whole town was in an uproar, and over at the Baptist church, a hasty meeting was called in the wee hours of the next morning. The Baptists had just built a new gymnasium that included additional classrooms for Sunday school, and it was the pride and joy of the congregation. By sundown, the decision had been made to offer the new facility to the Methodist church to use while their sanctuary was rebuilt. They accepted. For almost two years, the two congregations intermingled, sharing weddings, funerals, happy times, and sad—which continued even after the new church was completed.

Though the incident happened in the late 1970s, the two churches are still sharing their lives and hearts with one another as if it happened yesterday. Through tragedy, one church gave with no expectation of compensation, while the other gladly received with a grateful heart. Through this act, the hearts and minds of hundreds of people were changed, literally overnight, in a lasting, lifelong way.

Gratitude keeps you in a positive and open mind-set. It has a calming influence over your life and the lives of those you meet and associate with every day. Gratitude allows you to give to others, creating a flood of blessings and reward flowing back to you.

An excerpt from "The Prophet" by Kahlil Gibran

Then said a rich man, "Speak to us of Giving."
And he answered:

You give but little when you give of your possessions.
It is when you give of yourself that you truly give.

For what are your possessions but things
you keep and guard
for fear you may need them tomorrow?
And tomorrow, what shall tomorrow
bring to the over prudent dog
burying bones in the trackless sand as he follows the
pilgrims to the holy city?
And what is fear of need but need itself?
Is not dread of thirst when your well is full,
the thirst that is unquenchable?

There are those who give little
of the much which they have—
and they give it
for recognition and their hidden desire

makes their gifts unwholesome.
And there are those who have little and give it all.
These are the believers in life and the bounty of life,
and their coffer is never empty.
There are those who give with joy,
and their joy is their reward.
And there are those who give with pain,
and that pain is their baptism.
And there are those who give and know not
pain in giving, nor do they seek joy,
nor give with mindfulness of virtue:
They give as in yonder valley the myrtle
breathes its fragrance into space.
Through the hands of such as these God
speaks, and from behind their eyes
He smiles upon the earth.

It is well to give when asked, but it is
better to give unasked, through understanding:
And to the open-handed the search for
one who shall receive is joy greater than giving.
And is there aught you would withhold?
All you have shall some day be given:
Therefore give now, that the season of
giving may be yours and not your inheritors.

You often say, "I would give, but only to the deserving."
The trees in your orchard say not so,
nor the flocks in your pasture.
They give that they may live,
for to withhold is to perish.
Surely he who is worthy to receive his
days and nights, is worthy of all else from you.

And he who has deserved to drink from
the ocean of life deserves to fill his cup from your
little stream.
And what desert greater shall there be,
than that, which lies in the courage and the
confidence, nay the charity, of receiving?
And who are you that men should rend
their bosom and unveil their pride,
that you may see their worth naked and their pride
unabashed?
See first that you yourself deserve to be
a giver, and an instrument of giving.

For in truth it is life that gives unto life—while you, who
deem yourself a giver are but a witness.

And you receivers—and you are all
receivers—assume no weight of gratitude,
lest you lay a yoke upon
yourself and upon he who gives.
Rather rise together with the giver on his gifts as
on wings:
For to be over mindful of your debt, is
to doubt his generosity who has the
free-hearted earth for mother, and God for father.

We understand that change is inevitable and will come, whether we embrace it or not. But what many don't realize is that they have an active role in that change and can not only determine their own path, but they can create their own life. It almost sounds like you're playing God with your life, and you are. He gave us free will for a reason, and we can choose what we do, what we say, and how we live. If we don't like it, we can change it on the spot and try something else. None of us has a set pattern or formula we must follow.

[10]So the servants went out into the streets and gathered all the people they could find, both good and bad, and the wedding hall was filled with guests. [11]"But when the king came in to see the guests, he noticed a man there who was not wearing wedding clothes. [12]"Friend," he asked, "how did you get in here without wedding clothes?" The man was speechless. [13]"Then the king told the attendants, 'Tie him hand and foot, and throw him outside, into the darkness, where there will be weeping and gnashing of teeth.' [14]"For many are invited, but few are chosen." [15]Then the Pharisees went out and laid plans to trap him in his words. [16]They sent their disciples to him along with the Herodians. "Teacher," they said,

"we know you are a man of integrity and that you teach the way of God in accordance with the truth. You aren't swayed by men, because you pay no attention to who they are. [17]Tell us then, what is your opinion? Is it right to pay taxes to Caesar or not?" [18]But Jesus, knowing their evil intent, said, "You hypocrites, why are you trying to trap me? [19]Show me the coin used for paying the tax." They brought him a denarius, [20]and he asked them, "Whose portrait is this? And whose inscription?" [21]"Caesar's," they replied. Then he said to them, "Give to Caesar what is Caesar's, and to God what is God's."

–Matthew 22:10–21 (New International Version)

CHAPTER 37

THINKING CHANGE IS GOOD

> *You become what you think about.*
>
> **–Earl Nightingale and Aristotle**

I often see so many people who take themselves way too seriously. God never intended our lives to be perfect or he would not have created us the way he did. He intends our lives to be a comedy of errors as we find our way along the path of our choosing. One thing you don't hear near enough of in churches these days is laughter. Haven't you ever wondered about that? God created laughter, and there have been numerous times that I been in a truly surreal and weird situation where I've thought, "Is this for real or is God punkin' me again?"

You must be able to laugh at yourself and laugh at the various scenarios you encounter in your life. Laughter frees up your body and mind from cumulative stress—almost like unscrewing the valve on an overfilled tire. The pressure is released, and you can start anew with a more positive perspective.

The day Sheila and I met Art Linketter we had just returned from a trip to Alaska on Princess Cruiseline. We had a delightful time with Sheila's best friend, Lenoir Bunn, and her husband. The boat was Italian, and we decided that, being in Vancouver, we would sample the Chinese food there. We asked the concierge for directions to a Chinese restaurant. He recommended one close to the hotel. We arrived, and the maitre'd seated us. Sheila immediately got an unusual look on her face and said "Lynn, I think that's Art Linkletter sitting behind you." I looked around and said, "Hum ... I thought he was dead, but I believe you're right."

Sheila's grandmother, Rhoda Spong, was 98 at the time, and when Sheila was growing up, before she did her homework, she could watch Art Linkletter's *Kids Say the Darnedest Things*. She knew him well as a fan and also knew that her grandmother would love to have his autograph. The menu was not a fancy exclusive menu but rather a practical daily menu for the restaurant, and the only paper we had. I gave her the menu and the pen I had in my pocket. She went over and knelt down beside him and said, "I think I know who you are," and he smiled and immediately said, "I know you know who I am. I saw you watching me." She told him her story, and he looked over to me and waved. He was there with his wife.

Sheila came back to the table with Linkletter's autograph, and we ordered. We were halfway through our meal when they finished eating. They got up and came over to our table, and he introduced me to his wife. We chatted about their daughter and his efforts to help with young people to understand altered states of mind with drugs. He also encouraged us to go to Lake Louise. He and his wife left there and were going back home following their vacation in that part of Canada.

What a delightful open gentleman who obviously had never met a stranger. He and Mark Victor Hanson have written a marvelous book, *Make the Last Years of Your Life the Best Years of Your Life*. At 95, Art Linkletter continues to build businesses to have vacations with his large family of children, grandchildren, and great-grandchildren and continues to work to help others, making people laugh from birth to death. What a fantastic life of service to others.

If you've ever seen a celebrity wisked through an airport, most of us can only imagine what type of life that must be to be recognized everywhere. Watch television, and there is hardly a day that goes by that some famous actor, actress, or musician is not the target of media attention for personal issues that would cause most of us to shudder with embarrassment and outrage to be "outed" in such a way. Our society seems preoccupied with negativity and failure. Have you ever watched such a gossip report and felt good? Probably not. If you pay attention to issues such as wanting revenge or actually taking revenge, there may be a momentary feeling of relief or satisfaction, but the underlying emotion in there is not a good one, however you may label it.

Now think just for a moment about a time when you induced a fit of laughter in someone (yourself included). How did that make you feel? Though sensationalism sells, the feelings caused by bringing joy to someone, with a gift, a thought, a letter, or a fit of laughter, is so much healthier for us mentally, physically, and emotionally.

Bringing joy to others is in the service of God, whether it is trying to help alleviate the suffering of the sick or injured or visiting the lonely in hospitals, nursing homes, or orphanages, or "trapped" within their own homes or lives of solitude. Or you can simply make someone laugh. Laughter creates such a strong healing vibration. If you remember Linkletter's show, you can easily remember the intense laughter we all found at the innocent statements made by children.

It's important to remember that the thoughts you focus on will determine what you experience. To constantly worry and fret means that you can't enjoy all that life is bringing to you each and every day. Thoughts of joy manifest themselves as joy to you and others around you. The feelings and emotions you project out into the world come back to you several times over and will help you stay on the path toward a new and brighter future.

> [9]*Do not lie to each other, since you have taken off your old self with its practices* [10]*and have put on the new self, which is being renewed in knowledge in the image of its Creator.* [11]*Here there is no Greek or Jew, circumcised or uncircumcised, barbarian, Scythian, slave or free, but Christ is all, and is in all.*
>
> **–Colossians 3:9–11 (New International Version)**

CHAPTER 38

COMMUNICATING THE MESSAGE

Watch your thoughts, they become words. Watch your words, they become actions. Watch your actions, they become habits. Watch your habits, they become character. Watch your character, it becomes your destiny

–Frank Outlaw

As you change your life, you will want to tell others. One of the interesting things that happens to many people is that the ones they want to share these new ideas with most (friends and family) may react negatively. This is normal, as they are still living in their own comfort zone, and for them to see you moving a different direction causes them discomfort. In order not to be discouraged, you must learn when and how to communicate the wonderful things going on in your life, while understanding that not all will receive the message. A great example of this in the Bible is Paul.

The ability to communicate and relate to others was one of the areas that Paul excelled at. It would be easy to assume that because he was an educated and elite member of the Jewish community that he was respected, but that would not be so. Paul was very educated and articulate. He could argue theology with the best men of his day, yet this had no bearing on his abilities due to the fact that the majority of people he taught and preached to were Gentiles. He easily could have turned them away from his message if he had talked over their heads or took on the air of superiority. In fact, he did just the opposite, pointing out his own faults in front of them and letting people know he was human.

Paul had a great gift of being able to adjust his message to the particular audience, arguing in the legalistic language of the Sadducees when facing his Jewish persecutors who continually tried to arrest him after his conversion, or instructing a far-removed congregation of Gentiles in the simplest and easiest to understand terms. All the while, Paul guarded his own mind against pride or feelings of superiority. This is a wonderful example for us. It can be easy once you feel you have found the answers to want everyone else to see things the same way—but they won't. It takes time, patience, and the willingness to love that person right where they are in their life before they will hear your message.

Paul's encouragement to new Christians was to abandon the idea of "an eye for an eye" and instead pray for and love your enemies. Paul taught that God is the ultimate judge and justice will come to those who harm others in thought or deed. This was a vast departure from long-held beliefs of both the Jew and Gentiles, and coming from a man who formerly persecuted Christians, this got people's attention.

The idea of a loving God that people should emulate was also a new idea. The Old Testament is full of the dark deeds of man and the wrath of God—fire and brimstone, as many refer to it. The prevailing view of religion in Christ's day was that God was jealous, vengeful, and angry. People lived in fear of God rather than loving God.

Paul's message was so different that it attracted large numbers who wanted something different—just as today the idea of melding science and religion is attracting substantial interest. People of that time were tired of fearing God and living in dread that they might anger him. In his letter to the Corinthians, Paul wrote one of the simplest and most profound passages explaining what real love is. This passage is an example of Paul's gift to simply and succinctly convey a revolutionary idea:

> [1] *If I speak in the tongues of men and of angels, but have not love, I am only a resounding gong or a clanging cymbal.* [2] *If I have the gift of prophecy and can fathom all mysteries and all knowledge, and if I have a faith that can move mountains, but have not love, I am nothing.* [3] *If I give all I possess to the poor and surrender my body to the flames, but have not love, I gain nothing.*

> [4] *Love is patient, love is kind. It does not envy, it does not boast, it is not proud.* [5] *It is not rude, it is not self-seeking, it is not easily angered, it keeps no record of wrongs.* [6] *Love does not delight in evil but rejoices with the truth.* [7] *It always protects, always trusts, always hopes, always perseveres.*

> [8] *Love never fails. But where there are prophecies, they will cease; where there are tongues, they will be stilled; where there is knowledge, it will pass away.* [9] *For we know in part and we prophesy in part,* [10] *but when perfection comes, the imperfect disappears.* [11] *When I was a child, I talked like a child, I thought like a child, I reasoned*

like a child. When I became a man, I put childish ways behind me. [12] Now we see but a poor reflection as in a mirror; then we shall see face to face. Now I know in part; then I shall know fully, even as I am fully known.

[13] And now these three remain: faith, hope and love. But the greatest of these is love.

–1 Corinthians 13 (New International Version)

This passage is one of the most often quoted in the Bible as it touches the heart of the most learned to the most simple, and this was Paul's gift. The ability to bring the message to all people and cultures on their level allowed him to cross barriers no other disciple or apostle had been able to breach.

Paul's success in spreading the message of Christianity across much of the known world at the time was due to the perfect combination of his ability to communicate so strongly to each individual group with a message these people were ready to hear. The lesson for us is the understanding that even if we have a great message to tell, we must be able to communicate that message effectively or no one will listen. You must also hone your message to be sure it is one that your audience is ready to hear. This does not mean backing down from hard subject matter or hiding your thoughts, as that does no one any good. But it does mean critically evaluating your ideas and ensuring that what you are presenting is positive, uplifting, and of benefit to others.

As most of us have experienced personally and learned through the historical experiences of our ancestors, messages of hate eventually fail while messages of love create a better society and better world. Paul notes this in the first chapter of his letter to the Philippians after he was imprisoned:

[12] Now I want you to know, brothers, that what has happened to me has really served to advance the gospel. [13] As a result, it has become clear throughout the whole

palace guard and to everyone else that I am in chains for Christ. ¹⁴ *Because of my chains, most of the brothers in the Lord have been encouraged to speak the word of God more courageously and fearlessly.*

¹⁵ *It is true that some preach Christ out of envy and rivalry, but others out of goodwill.* ¹⁶ *The latter do so in love, knowing that I am put here for the defense of the gospel.* ¹⁷ *The former preach Christ out of selfish ambition, not sincerely, supposing that they can stir up trouble for me while I am in chains.* ¹⁸ *But what does it matter? The important thing is that in every way, whether from false motives or true, Christ is preached. And because of this I rejoice.*

Yes, and I will continue to rejoice, ¹⁹ *for I know that through your prayers and the help given by the Spirit of Jesus Christ, what has happened to me will turn out for my deliverance.* ²⁰ *I eagerly expect and hope that I will in no way be ashamed, but will have sufficient courage so that now as always Christ will be exalted in my body, whether by life or by death.* ²¹ *For to me, to live is Christ and to die is gain.* ²² *If I am to go on living in the body, this will mean fruitful labor for me. Yet what shall I choose? I do not know!* ²³ *I am torn between the two: I desire to depart and be with Christ, which is better by far;* ²⁴ *but it is more necessary for you that I remain in the body.* ²⁵ *Convinced of this, I know that I will remain, and I will continue with all of you for your progress and joy in the faith,* ²⁶ *so that through my being with you again your joy in Christ Jesus will overflow on account of me.*

²⁷ Whatever happens, conduct yourselves in a manner worthy of the gospel of Christ. Then, whether I come and see you or only hear about you in my absence, I will know that you stand firm in one spirit, contending as one man for the faith of the gospel ²⁸ without being frightened in any way by those who oppose you. This is a sign to them that they will be destroyed, but that you will be saved— and that by God. ²⁹ For it has been granted to you on behalf of Christ not only to believe on him, but also to suffer for him, ³⁰ since you are going through the same struggle you saw I had, and now hear that I still have.

–Philippians 1:12–30

Another notable fact about Paul is that his daily life reflected what he preached and wrote. Christ was his example in this. The teacher or messenger who is willing to live among the people and experience their problems has much more influence on them. They see him every day endure the same problems, persecutions, and issues of everyday life and can see how he handles them. This doesn't mean Paul was perfect; he wasn't, but he did not try to hide that fact and reminded his followers often of his own person shortcomings. This is a good lesson for us as we strive to improve our experience and understanding. We aren't perfect, and none of us have the exact right answers, but we are all learning and growing, and that is what matters. We will stumble at times and even fail, but as long as we are willing to support others in their time of need, they will support us.

¹ When I came to you, brothers, I did not come with eloquence or superior wisdom as I proclaimed to you the testimony about God. ² For I resolved to know nothing while I was with you except Jesus Christ and him crucified. ³ I came to you in weakness and fear, and with much trembling. ⁴ My message and my preaching

*were not with wise and persuasive words, but with a
demonstration of the Spirit's power, ⁵ so that your faith
might not rest on men's wisdom, but on God's power.*

⁶ *We do, however, speak a message of wisdom among the
mature, but not the wisdom of this age or of the rulers
of this age, who are coming to nothing. ⁷ No, we speak of
God's secret wisdom, a wisdom that has been hidden and
that God destined for our glory before time began. ⁸ None
of the rulers of this age understood it, for if they had, they
would not have crucified the Lord of glory. ⁹ However, as
it is written: "No eye has seen, no ear has heard, no mind
has conceived what God has prepared for those who love
him" ¹⁰ but God has revealed it to us by his Spirit.*

*The Spirit searches all things, even the deep things of
God. ¹¹ For who among men knows the thoughts of a
man except the man's spirit within him? In the same
way no one knows the thoughts of God except the Spirit
of God. ¹² We have not received the spirit of the world
but the Spirit who is from God, that we may understand
what God has freely given us. ¹³ This is what we speak,
not in words taught us by human wisdom but in words
taught by the Spirit, expressing spiritual truths in
spiritual words. ¹⁴ The man without the Spirit does not
accept the things that come from the Spirit of God, for
they are foolishness to him, and he cannot understand
them, because they are spiritually discerned. ¹⁵ The
spiritual man makes judgments about all things, but
he himself is not subject to any man's judgment: ¹⁶
"For who has known the mind of the Lord that he may
instruct him?" But we have the mind of Christ.*

–1 Corinthians 2:1–16 (New International Version)

It may seem a little odd that Paul works so hard in this passage to convince the congregation that he does not do this to glorify himself or prop himself up. At the time, there were other teachers trying to pull the Christians toward their faction and beliefs. These men were the snake oil salesmen of their time, leading people astray and trying to gain control of their own group of believers.

Paul set himself apart as a servant, which was unusual in that day—as it is in our own. So many people you see selling products on late-night TV are not doing so to help others, and it is very evident. They come across as slick and pushy, and they are because their motivation doesn't resonate with their audience. However, when you hear a speaker, teacher, or coach speak to you on your own terms, right where you are in your life, and their desire is for you to learn what they know for no other reason than to improve your own life, you know it and feel it—just as the early Christians did with Paul.

⁸Finally, all of you, live in harmony with one another; be sympathetic, love as brothers, be compassionate and humble. ⁹Do not repay evil with evil or insult with insult, but with blessing, because to this you were called so that you may inherit a blessing. ¹⁰For, "Whoever would love life and see good days must keep his tongue from evil and his lips from deceitful speech. ¹¹He must turn from evil and do good; he must seek peace and pursue it. ¹²For the eyes of the Lord are on the righteous and his ears are attentive to their prayer, but the face of the Lord is against those who do evil."

–1 Peter 3:8–12 (New International Version)

CHAPTER 39

40 WEEKS TO LASTING CHANGE

Our greatest glory is not in never falling, but in rising every time we fall.

–Confucius

Change is a process that builds on previous efforts. It is not instantaneous, in most cases, and it won't last without constant vigilance. As many a great philosopher has lamented, the first step is always the hardest, but if you never take it, you never succeed.

The first step for anyone wanting to improve his or her life, health, finances, or faith is to honestly evaluate where he or she is. This means taking a good look at what you consider your strengths and weaknesses. I caution you not to overload on weaknesses, as this is a common tendency. Remember, the Law of Polarity states that for everything there is an opposite, so you should have strength for each weakness—they are never out of balance. Write this list down and set it aside for a few days and then come back to it and see if you've thought of others to add.

Now make a list of what you want. What dreams do you have or have had in the past? You can use the right-brained writing exercises to help with this and do them over the course of at least one week. Once you have that list created, make a list of why those things haven't come to pass. What obstacles do you perceive are standing in your way?

Once you have made your lists, go to a close friend or family member. Don't share your lists with them, but ask for their honest opinion on what they think your strengths and weaknesses are and what improvements they think you should make in your life. It is interesting that often those closest to us see us more objectively than we see ourselves, but we rarely ask for their help or take their advice when it's offered. This time listen and write it down. This is not a time for rebuttal or disagreement. Accept everything they say and then think on the truth of it when you get home and compare it to your own list.

Now that you've made your lists and thought about them a while, make a list of changes you want to make in each area of your life, finances, health, personal growth, spirituality, and any other categories you choose. Prioritize the list. You now have a prioritized list of the items in your life you wish to change.

Now set your goals for the next 40 weeks. These goals must be specific and definable with a good time attached so that you can measure your progress. Take the top goal in each category and put one step that you will take in each category this week—write this on your first week.

Here is an example:

Kevin feels that his top priorities are:

- Getting a better job

- Losing twenty pounds

- Repairing a tense relationship with his father

- Planning a vacation to Europe

Kevin noted on his obstacle list that he felt the fact that he doesn't have a degree inhibits his ability to get a better job. So this week he notes that he will set up a time to speak with a local academic advisor to see what is available for night and weekend classes.

Kevin was athletic in school but now gets no exercise. So this week Kevin sets the goal to spend his lunch hour walking around the block where his office is located.

Kevin's relationship has been tense with his father for years due to Kevin dropping out of college rather than finishing. Kevin isn't ready to contact his father, but he commits to himself that he will spend a few minutes each day writing out the things he likes most about his dad and the type of relationship he would like them to have. This is very much like visualizing your outcome before it happens. It also softens Kevin's own heart so that when he does talk to his dad, it will be a nonconfrontational encounter on his part.

Kevin has assumed for years that he couldn't afford to go to Europe. This week he commits to talking to some travel agents and finding out if there are inexpensive ways to see Europe and exactly how much it really does cost so that he'll have a number to work with.

Now Kevin has his first week planned with four items. You may have more than four, you may have less, but the idea is to write them down, start the process, and track them.

You may think that doing something for 40 weeks is a big commitment, but really it's not. You are committing to do it for one week, and once you feel the victory from accomplishing the list for that week, then you commit to the next week. This is how change really works. It's not a huge life-altering commitment; it's one step at a time, one day at a time, one week at a time, until these behaviors and goals manifest into reality.

As you work through this process, there are a few things that can cause you to stumble. One of those is comparing yourself to others. We always like to relate ourselves in comparison to others, almost like an unconscious ranking system. As if we are constantly asking, "Am I better than them?" For the most part, this is detrimental as it gives us a distorted perspective. For example, I once knew a boy who was in an elite prep school. He shared that he felt that he was stupid. I knew that his grade point was near perfect and was astounded that he would so underestimate his intelligence. On further questioning, he said that the school had ranked his class, and he was near the bottom, which was still far above more than 90 percent of students in a nonprep environment. This was comparison at its worst.

The problem with comparison is that is doesn't measure us to an objective benchmark but rather compares our progress en route. This means that we are always dealing with moving targets that cannot be quantified and are therefore perfectly useless. The only benchmark you should use is your own, not your family's or friend's. You set the goals, and you decide when they are met, no one else. It makes no difference if ten other people with similar goals reach theirs before you. It's not a race against other people; it's a battle with yourself, and you can move at whatever pace you desire.

Just remember that you can do anything for a week and let the rest go. Don't worry about next week or next month. Only think of today and what you will accomplish and then give yourself kudos when you do.

> [22]Blessed are you when men hate you, when they exclude you and insult you and reject your name as evil, because of the Son of Man. [23]"Rejoice in that day and leap for joy, because great is your reward in heaven. For that is how their fathers treated the prophets.
>
> –Luke 6:22–23 (New International Version)

CHAPTER 40

YOUR BIRTHRIGHT

It's not the strongest of species that survive nor the most intelligent, but the most responsive to change

–Charles Darwin

You deserve to live an empowered life. This includes the areas of good health, financial stability, love, and knowledge. Within this book, I have shown that factions such as religion and science are not really separate, but part of the same universe we all share. As spiritual beings, we are free to try new ideas and test new areas of faith. As logical thinkers, we are also to acknowledge and embrace the advances of science. The true message of Jesus was love our neighbor as ourselves and serve the needs of those around us.

Notice, he didn't say we have to understand everyone or enable those who prey on others, but he said "love." Love begets joy, and with true joy in your heart, the circumstances of life matter little. We put much time and energy into things that don't matter. If you awake in spirit tomorrow to discover you had died, what would matter? That new Mercedes in the driveway, or the fact that you'd never even spoken to your next-door neighbor? Would you feel the same outrage you did the day before when someone called Baptists snake charmers? No. Once all the clutter is stripped away, there are few things that matter and few things more vital than the people we have relationships with.

Christ spent his whole life and death to get across the message that all these external things we deem important are insignificant in the big picture. The idea that someone might be put to death for saying the world is flat seems ridiculous to us, but it shows how obsessed we can become as humans to prove we have the answers.

By discovering and implementing the principles and ideas in this work into daily life, you will create an awareness that you may not have previously experienced prior to absorbing this new knowledge, which the author has now proved is actually ancient understanding reinvented. It is important to understand that it is in the implementation of the knowledge acquired through this book, and learning to harmonize your actions with their unwavering certainty, that will allow and enable you to experience a life above and beyond your wildest expectations.

[1]Therefore, I urge you, brothers, in view of God's mercy, to offer your bodies as living sacrifices, holy and pleasing to God—this is your spiritual act of worship. [2]Do not conform any longer to the pattern of this world, but be transformed by the renewing of your mind. Then you will be able to test and approve what God's will is—his good, pleasing and perfect will. [3]For by the grace given me I say to every one of you: Do not think of yourself more highly than you ought, but rather think of yourself with sober judgment, in accordance with the measure of faith God has given you.

–Romans 12:1–3 (New International Version)

ABOUT THE AUTHOR

Dr. Lynn Hughes, MD, MTS, Awakened and Aware

Jesus said, "Let the little children come to me, and do not hinder them, for the kingdom of heaven belongs to such as these."

–Matthew 19:13–15

A Child of Jehovah, A Subject of Grace

11s

A Child of Jehovah, A subject of grace,
I'm of the seed royal, a dignified race,
An heir of salvation, redeemed with blood,
I'll own my relation, my Father is God!

He loved me of old, and he loveth me still
Before the creation, he gave me by will,
A portion worth more than the Indes of gold,
Which cannot be wasted, nor mortgaged nor sold.

He gave me a Surety, a covenant Head
To live in my name, and to die in my stead,
He gave me a righteousness wholly divine,
And viewed all the merits of Jesus as mine.

He gave a Perceptor infallibly wise,
And treasures of grace to be send in supplies;
Yea, all that I ask for my Father hath given.
To help me on Earth, and to crown me in heav'n.

He gave me a will to accept what he gave,
Though I was averse to his purpose to save;
He wrote in his will my repentance and faith,
And all my enjoyments for life and for death.

My trails and sorrows, my comforts and cares
The spirit of prayer and the answer of prayers
The steps that I tread, and the station I fill,
My Father determined and wrote in his will.

My cross and my crown are both willed by my God,
He swore to his will, and then sealed it with blood.
'Tis proved by the Spirit, the witness within,
'Tis mine to inherit, I'll glory begin.

This is the story of my journey in life and awareness of the support for rather than rejection of the Success Movement in Christian Scripture, both Old Testament and the New Testament. I feel that my life of study, including my youth as the child of an enlightened Baptist minister, earning a master's degree in theological studies, and the successful completion of medical school, leading to not only a medical practice but also a ministry of serving those less fortunate in underdeveloped countries, has empowered me to draw my own conclusions, which are presented in this book. I hope to show just how I came to reconcile religion, spirituality, and most importantly, the understanding of various human paths and beliefs that all strive for the same end—to know God and arrive at eternal life with "him." And I hope you, my reader, will gain insight how to best do the same in your own life.

When I was six years old, one night I awakened my mother and father, feeling that I wanted to be saved and become a Christian. My father, a Baptist minister, got up and along with my mother consoled me and read to me John 3:16. I became a believer and was baptized by immersion in the First Baptist Church in Ardmore, Oklahoma.

I lived in Ardmore until I was a junior in high school. My father was raised a farmer and felt the call to be a minister when he was in a one-room school in the country near Adair, Oklahoma. He became the first college graduate in his family at Oklahoma Baptist University. His father and relatives began the church at Pleasant Hope in the late 1800s before Oklahoma became a state. His mother's relatives were Trail of Tears Cherokee Indians from North Georgia. Fortunately, good family records were kept, so I was able to trace and claim my Cherokee ancestry.

As an associational missionary, my father assisted in the building of many churches. He was instrumental in beginning four new churches in the Ardmore, Oklahoma, area. Needless to say, my younger brother and I worked together with Dad, building these churches. We learned many trades—plumbing, sheet rocking, painting, wallpapering, asbestos siding, roofing, framing, digging foundations, keeping yards, finish carpentry, and about everything that can be done in building of churches and repair of buildings at that time. My brother and I could do this work - including repairing the gas stoves that were used for heating.

We regularly attended two to three weeks at Falls Creek Baptist Assembly, which continues to be a large gathering of Baptists in Oklahoma. Several thousand people from multiple churches gather for a week of worship, relaxation, and sharing. It was there at a Royal Ambassador camp that I felt the call for missions, without specifics, but it opened my eyes to other possibilities career-wise. Dr. James Hobson Veazy was our delightful family doctor who made house calls and loved children. I think he took care of ministers gratis at the time. We always gave him a gift at Christmas, and he was always very gracious and grateful for our gifts. This directed me to consider medicine as a career.

During the time I was at home, my father put together a vacation schedule so that we could spend three weeks together—one week for continuing education at the Southern Baptist Convention or Glorietta location for learning followed by a traveling vacation. We would begin by driving through the South through Louisiana, Mississippi, Alabama, Georgia, and down to Florida for the Southern Baptist Convention in Miami. We left Miami and drove up the coast to see Washington DC, on up to New York, and then up as far as Maine before returning to Oklahoma.

Dad had rigged our 1954 Chevrolet station wagon so that we could sleep in it or on top of it and carry all of our belongings so that we did not require a motel. We had a great time and were introduced to the eastern part of the country first, and then we went west to Glorietta, New Mexico, for a Baptist retreat. Following the retreat, we went to Arizona, including the Grand Canyon, and on to California, where we visited San Diego, Los Angeles, and up to San Francisco. From San Francisco, we looped back through Reno, Nevada, and then through Utah and Colorado before returning finally to Oklahoma. What a trip!

 The next year we went to Mexico. We did stay in motels when we went down into Mexico with a Spanish-speaking friend—my father's roommate's son, who introduced us to the foreign country. We visited many cities, learned some Spanish, and most importantly, we gained an appreciation for the people and the culture.

In 1955, my father felt a call to begin a church in Tulsa, Oklahoma. What a shift that was for our family with the children going from a school of 100 graduates per class to a school of 1,500 graduates per class in a city of 150,000 from a city of 10,000. It was a major growing experience. My brother and I began sharpening our skills in the building of this church, made new friends, and prepared for college—of course, Oklahoma Baptist University.

A TIME FOR LEARNING

My father, a Baptist minister, was also raised on a farm. He became the first son in the Hughes family to go to college and finish a degree. He taught school initially then went to OBU and taught high school in Adair, Oklahoma, in a one-room schoolhouse near where his sister lived. He went to Southwestern Baptist Theological Seminary next, where he met my mother. After obtaining his bachelor of divinity degree, he moved to Ardmore, Oklahoma, where the four children, my three siblings, and I were born. He was a fantastic father and pastor, and he started five different churches in Ardmore. He built all of them basically by hand, with the help of local people in the church who had some carpentry, painting, and electrical or plumbing skills. When my brother John and I were 5 and 7 years old, we began to work with our father building churches. By the time I was 12 and my brother was 10, we were fairly skilled at plumbing, connecting gas stoves, doing the old-fashioned lead filling for toilets and water heaters and baptisteries, painting the windows, ceilings, roofing—we could do it all.

By the time my brother and I were 16 and 14, it was probably time that we needed to be saving some money and working for others. My father had given us the skills that were required to work to pay for college. Dad suggested we seek a scholarship at Oklahoma Baptist University. We also were able to pay for our education, my seminary education, my brother's dental education, and my medical school.

In the summer of 1961, I had graduated from Oklahoma Baptist University in three and a half years and started working on a master's degree in philosophy from the University of Oklahoma, taking six hours of philosophy while I was working to support myself. I also took an English class, giving me full-time status in school, which meant my low draft number was still pending.

At that time, your draft number was your ticket to Vietnam. Class I-S was a student deferred by law until graduation from high school or attainment of the age of 20, or until end of his academic year at a college or university. Class IV-D was a minister of religion or divinity student.

I had no possibility, as I saw it, to avoid the draft unless I could get accepted to another school acceptable to the government for deferment. After graduation from college and with the low draft number, I had sent in an application to Ohio State University where I could go ahead and continue as a full-time student, but I found out that the deferment for master degrees in philosophy did not count as a potential deferment. That being the case, because I was not already accepted to medical school and had not evaluated the possibility of theology or divinity school, I sat down and talked with my father about what my options were. He was not going to permit me to go to school locally in Ohio with room and board. He suggested that I go to Southwestern Baptist Theological Seminary in Fort Worth, Texas, where he had gone to school, especially since I had considered a career as a medical missionary and would require a theology degree before I would be able to go anywhere as a missionary for the Southern Baptist Church. After thinking about my options for a couple weeks, I applied to the Southwestern Baptist Theological Seminary and was accepted as a candidate for a degree in theology; at that time it was a bachelor's of divinity. I was subsequently accepted and began theology school at Southwestern Baptist Theological Seminary and got my deferment from the immediate draft.

I worked in multiple job positions while I was in the seminary and managed to work on cars at one point. Finally I got a job in a laboratory in Fort Worth, Texas, and was able to pay for my education through that job in the laboratory and the office of a pathologist. Because of the female pathologist who was in charge of the lab, I got good hours and good pay and began moving in the direction of medical school. After my first year of theology school, I worked with my uncle one summer, helping him to build a cabin, and was able to visit my grandparents who lived not far from Fort Worth on the weekends when I was not working.

Also after the first year, I had an opportunity to go to the islands of the Caribbean, specifically the Bahamas, and while there, I was part of a group of about seven seminary students who went to hold Vacation Bible Schools and to assist working with the people of the islands. We all got very well acquainted with the capital of the Bahamas and with several students in the Bahamas who were also assisting with the Vacation Bible School in the outer islands. One gentleman with whom we spent much time and who became cohort for the Bahamas taught me a lot about different cultures. We were able to deal with these cultural variances in a very good way, learning how different people live in the world, which was a great opportunity. After the summer in the Bahamas, we brought one local woman back with us, and I learned about our country's culture in the process.

We came in through Miami; she had a passport and had been in the United States before. I had never traveled in the United States in the South with a black person. We found out quickly that she was not welcome at the bathrooms at the local service stations. There was a bathroom in the back for black people. That was an eye opener for me. She was aware of that and knew that she had to use separate facilities. She parted company with us and went on her way to be with her family and other family members after we got her to Atlanta. The rest of our group returned to Fort Worth.

During the time I was in the Bahamas, I felt that my life's purpose was to be a physician, and I started discussing it with other people that were there in the mission field and contemplated the possibility of getting into medical school. I talked with some of my friends who were already in medical school, and they said they knew that I would have no problem doing the same. I had been told that after my sophomore year of college, when I had straight C's, that the courses that I thought were vital to medical school would be impossible for me to get into. I went to the advisor for the medical school for Oklahoma Baptist University who was a Chinese professor of biology. I had taken a biology course with him and asked him when I had the straight C's what I was going to be able to do about getting into medical school as the two C's had occurred when we went home for Christmas holidays and the final exams were after we returned. I had studied and had been doing well in the courses, but the first love of my life decided that she was going to marry her hometown boyfriend. Even though we had talked on the phone and were in our respective homes, she came back with a ring from him, which crushed this 19-year-old college student.

My grades suffered heavily because I was not able to put things together at that time. The advisor said he didn't think I would be able to get into medical school with my grades. He suggested that I needed to change my major to something I really liked. Well, I changed it to study English and philosophy. I already had enough coursework to have a minor in math and chemistry so that permitted and fostered a period of study, maturity, and learning about life.

I had discovered on my own with the free time I had at the Vacation Bible Schools in the Bahamas to know that I had been led astray by the Chinese professor, and I had not done due diligence about getting into medical school. When I returned from the Bahamas, I immediately called the University of Oklahoma School of Medicine, which was the only one I could afford, and I was told that all I needed was two courses in physics with good grades to go ahead with my application. I immediately enrolled in a night course in physics at Texas Christian University. I finished both courses and then I took the MCAT and passed. Then I applied to medical school. Subsequently I had to go to Oklahoma City for an interview for medical school on a Thursday evening.

At the time of the interview, we had five interviewees each with a 30-minute interview. It was interesting in that one of the interviewees was Dr. Ishmael. His immediate question to us was, "Who was Ishmael in the Bible?" I said he was Isaac's brother, the firstborn of Hagar, the handmaiden to Sarah, Abraham's wife. He congratulated me for being aware of that. Obviously I had studied theology, though not from a Jewish perspective. Later that evening, as we left, I was called aside with the person I had been discussing medical school with. He made me aware that the committee had voted that I had been accepted into medical school for the next year. What a fantastic relief. I then visited some other friends and found a place to stay for the first year.

I returned to Ft. Worth to finish the last courses I needed for graduation. It was right before graduation that I had an interesting experience with administration at the seminary. They discovered at the end of my third year when I was just about to complete my degree that I had taken the course in physics for four hours. At the same time I had taken 17 and 18 hours of theology, which gave me a total of 21 and 22 hours for credit. The Texas

Christian University and Southwestern Baptist Theological Seminary had an agreement that if they had any students that were studying at both schools that there could not be more than 18 hours total. However, the evening courses were not a part of it, and so that permitted me to be a full-time student at Southwestern Baptist Theological Seminary and a part-time student at TCU since it was at night. The person in charge said several things could happen. He could not sign off on obtaining the degree. He asked, "What kind of grades did you make?" I said I had an A-average. I got A's at TCU, I got A's and B's at the seminary. He said, "You're right, it doesn't make either of us look very good for you to have this kind of grades with 22 and 21 hours of credit." He thought for a minute and said that because I had already been accepted to medical school, it made little or no difference. I said thank you very much, and then I left. I got my degree in theology and then got my deferment for medical school next.

With the laboratory skills that I picked up while I was in seminary school, I was able to work during medical school in the chemistry laboratory, which was one of the best jobs for a student because even if you had to do five, six, or seven tests for chemistry, it only took me about 20 minutes from the time I was awake to go do the test, and I was able to be back in bed in about 30 minutes. In the blood laboratory, however, you took tests for an hour because you had to wait for certain things that couldn't be done at the same time. It took a full hour and if you had a real bleeder or someone who needed a lot of blood transfusions, it could require the whole night. This was a blessing for me to be able to do that work. We also donated bone marrow for experimentation purposes.

We sometimes slept in the sleep lab where they measured what certain medications did to our brains while we were asleep. We did that multiple times. During my junior year, I got an opportunity to help the faculty club. At that time, Oklahoma was a dry state. The faculty club was where the faculty gathered together to have a drink after a long day. They also had guest rooms in the faculty club where visiting professors could have a room of their own, so someone had to be there 24 hours a day. That was no problem during the day and evening because a lot of people came to eat breakfast, dinner, and lunch. There were three of us who needed a place to stay: students Chang and Marvell and me.

We stayed in the faculty club for two years and basically were not paid much, but we were allowed to eat any extra food and feed eight to ten guys periodically the leftover soup and sandwiches from the day before that were still good. We only had to purchase food when the faculty club was closed. We got a meal the night we were on call and all the leftovers before they were thrown out. Especially due to our lifestyles, it was good to be able to sleep and eat in the same place. That gave us much more time for scheduled medical activities. It turned out being fantastic. I also moved on.

I married Jeannie, the mother of my daughters Shannon and Heather, in the middle of my junior year in Alexandria, Virginia. We then moved to a home in Dell City near Tinker Air Force Base where Jeannie worked. After I completed my rotating internship, we then volunteered to serve our time in the military; service seemed inevitable with my low draft number. My total debt at the end of medical school was the cost of the engagement ring for Jeannie, which was about $500. I did get paid during the internship, which included two months of dermatology, two months of anesthesiology, two months of psychiatry, two months in medicine, two months in the emergency room, and two months in surgery. As we neared the end of the internship, but before we finished it, we arranged through Jeannie's dad, Major General Johnson, who was well connected at the Pentagon, to be initially assigned to the army, but because his daughter was in the air force, he then assisted us in making arrangements for us to get a commission to move to the air force and for me to become a flight surgeon in the air force. This gave me an opportunity to see the world.

We had a super opportunity between my sophomore and junior years in medical school to go to Vietnam as a representative of the State Department. We did this as volunteers and were paid room and board and travel expenses to go work and study with Vietnamese medical students in Saigon for three months. Before we arrived, the program kind of fell apart a bit because a medical student in Vietnam emolliated himself, and with that occurrence it was felt that it was not the best time to be there. So each one of the five medical students between their sophomore and junior years were at different schools, five of us were assigned to military prevental health assistant teams, and that summer I actually became the AKBK (above the knee below the knee) amputation expert.

I had been taught to do chest tubes by the surgeon on one occasion, and after that, I became the expert in applying chest tubes for shrapnel injuries while they were treating other people who had been injured more severely. Chest tubes are inserted into the chest cavity's pleural space to either release blood or air so that the lung can again expand fully after an injury. Done incorrectly, the lung itself can be damaged. One night I put in seven chest tubes after the diagnosis was made by the internal medicine MD. This was just one occasion in my life when I learned quickly to do something that would normally cause fear, but because I did it and had the confidence in myself and faith that God would help me be the best at what I do, I moved forward in faith and was able to quickly improve my medical skills and grow as a person.

I returned to medical school having done more surgery than I witnessed in my first surgical rotation back at medical school. As I came back, I elected to travel back through Europe and reported one day late to my junior year in medical school, having been a marvelous witness of the plight of people in Southeast Asia and their problems but with the full knowledge of the fact that we did not belong there.

To this day, I frequently travel with other physicians to underprivileged countries to help those in need any way I can. In part, as I have gotten to know different people, cultures, and religions around the world, the idea for this book took form. I didn't realize it at first, as I was on my own quest of personal discovery to learn how to blend the scientific facts I knew with the religious beliefs I'd been taught and learned throughout my life. As I found my own personal truth, I developed a deep desire to share these discoveries with others, and now I have done so with this book.

I speak and teach people in many venues and situations as I have for years, and this tool allows me to reach even more. It is my fondest hope that every reader will follow his or her own path to discover his or her own truths and live the most fulfilled and meaningful life possible.

APPENDIX:

7 Super Laws of Quantum Physics

		Reference Pages
Law 1:	The Law of Perpetual Transmutation of Energy	9, 41, 144
Law 2:	The Law of Vibration	41, 42
	Subset: Law of Attraction	112, 113, 148
Law 3:	The Law of Relativity	11, 42, 50, 119, 144
Law 4:	The Law of Polarity	107
Law 5:	The Law of Rhythm	131, 132
Law 6:	The Law of Cause and Effect	126
Law 7:	The Law of Gestation or Gender	109, 135, 137, 158
The Extended Laws of Quantum Physics:		50

1. Giving

2. Gratitude

3. Accountability

4. Partnerships

5. Vision

6. Paradigms

UNDERSTANDING - SOURCE LIST

Pew Forum on Religion and Public Life (www.pewforum.org).

Ehrman, Bart D. *The Lost Christianities: The Battle for Scripture and the Faiths We Never Knew.*

Melancthon, Philip. A *History of the Life and Actions of the Very Reverend Dr. Martin Luther.*

Holliwell, Raymond. *Working with the Law.*

Newton, Sir Isaac. *Principia.*

Wolfe, Fred Allen. *Taking the Quantum Leap: The New Physics for Non-Scientists.*

Assaraf, John. "How the Brain Works." In *John Assaraf: More Money. More Life. More Love.* www.johnassaraf.com/blog/2009/04/24/how-the-brain-works.

Lipton, Bruce. *The Biology of Belief: Unleashing the Power of Consciousness, Matter, and Miracles.*

Einstein, Albert. *The World As I See It.*

Canfield, Jack. *Dream Big: Living the Law of Attraction.* Home study course. Santa Barbara, CA: Santa Barbara Wellness Institute.

Assaraf, John. *The Power of Meditation.*

Gladwell, Malcolm. *The Tipping Point.*

Canfield, Jack. *The Success Principles.*

Maltz, Maxwell. *Psycho-Cybernetics.*

INDEX

B

baptism, 68

Barth, Karl, 52

Basilica, 66

behavior, 247

beliefs

    creation. See Creation

    and paradigms, 252–253

    self-fulfilled, 231

Bethlehem town, 30

Bible, 25, 51

    formation of earth and cosmos, 78

    interpretation of Genesis, 58

    Law of Gestation and Gender, 196–197

Big Bang, 58

Biology of Belief: Unleashing the Power of Consciousness, Matter, and Miracles, The (Lipton), 114, 133

body

    functions of, 230

    and mind, 72, 88, 176

    taking care of, 162

birthright, 69, 290

Bohr, Niels, 106–107

Book of Esther, 182

Books of Moses, 31. See also Torah

brain, 20, 104

    functions of, 232

    left hemisphere, 231–232

    meditation, effect on, 175–176

    performing skill, 247

Empedocles, 61

energy, 61. See also Law of Perpetual Transmutation of Energy; theory of relativity

light as, 106, 113

thoughts as, 72, 154

enlightenment, 47, 66

Ephesians 1:11 (New International Version), 163

Essenes, 31, 224

ethical culture, intention of, 116

events, pattern of, 233–234

examples, and Christian life, 166

exercise, 162

Exodus, 146

"an eye for an eye," 30, 153, 238, 274

F

failure

experience of, 168

success without, 136. See also Law of Polarity

faith

definition of, 166–167

Einstein's view, 116

evolution of, 166–170

Goddard's message, 105

and gratitude, 169–170

and leadership, 170

Martin Luther's concept of, 68–69

misdirected, 167

Paul's message, 105

fear, 73

H

I

K

Q

S

T

U